CRITICALLY ACCLAIMED

THIS IS A GENUINE VIREO BOOK

A Vireo Book | Rare Bird Books
453 South Spring Street, Suite 302
Los Angeles, CA 90013
rarebirdbooks.com

Set in Minion
Printed in the United States

10 9 8 7 6 5 4 3 2 1

Publisher's Cataloging-in-Publication data
Names: Stradal, J. Ryan, editor. | Cushman, Adam, editor.
Title: Critically acclaimed / edited by J. Ryan Stradal and Adam Cushman.
Description: First Trade Paperback Original Edition | A Vireo Book | New York, NY;
Los Angeles, CA: Rare Bird Books, 2017.
Identifiers: ISBN 9781945572548
Subjects: LCSH Film criticism—Fiction. | Motion picture industry—Fiction. | Hollywood
(Los Angeles, Calif.)—Fiction. | Satire. | Humorous fiction. | BISAC FICTION / Satire |
FICTION / Humorous / General
Classification: LCC PS3603.R5795 S77 2017 | DDC 813.6—dc23

CRITICALLY ACCLAIMED

EDITED BY J. RYAN STRADAL WITH ADAM CUSHMAN

A GENUINE RARE BIRD BOOK LOS ANGELES, CALIF.

CONTENTS

KEVIN WILSON

THE ESSENTIAL FAILURE OF THE UNIVERSE

Directed by Naylon Beauregard. Starring: Angelina Jolie, Toni Collette, Jude Law, Jada Pinkett-Smith, Tom Cruise, Matt Damon, Laurence Fishburne, Zhang Ziyi, Robert Duvall, and Jason Robards as the president of the United States.

THERE ARE FEW THINGS that end up being worth the wait, the gradual buildup of expectation until it outpaces whatever the final product could ever become. And, yet, *Essential Target* was poised to top even our own outsized hopes. The pedigree suggested as much. Writer and director Naylon Beauregard's previous movie, *Acceleration Homeward*, netted just shy of $900 million in foreign and domestic box office totals. That film, an epic story of an entire civilization's lifespan aboard a spaceship the size of a planet, revitalized the sci-fi genre and made stars of Jude Law and Toni Collette. It changed the way special effects can enter the storytelling process, reminded us how a singular vision can speak to so many people, and, most importantly, altered our perceptions of our place in this universe. It was, to say the least, as life-changing as film can be. *Essential Target*, I must confess, does not succeed as a film in any traditional (or even nontraditional) sense of the form. It is so ponderous and overwhelmingly large in its focus that our current screens simply cannot accommodate it. I sense that, even if a screen were made that encapsulated the entire dome of the sky, it would not do justice to the aims of this film. What the film does accomplish, through means that may or may not revolve around the act of filmmaking, is to once again cause us to question our necessity in the universe, our need to exist, our possible movement toward a deserved extinction.

It's impossible to critique *Essential Target* without first addressing the issue surrounding its creation: the budget. What began as a $100-million movie turned into a $200-million movie and, by the time a quarter of a billion dollars had been spent on a single motion picture still not even half-finished, there seemed no option but to continue pouring money into what seemed to be the literal assembling of an entirely new reality. The final budget has not been released, but rumors put it at $2.5 billion. A large portion of this money, we of course have now learned, was put toward the scientific enterprise of discovering a new planet in the solar system and then—no other way to describe it—blowing it up. It seems pointless, in a film review, to discuss the ethical questions of this endeavor, only to relate how that experience, captured on film in astonishingly beautiful and disturbing detail, affects the experience of viewing the finished film.

The story concerns a committee of world leaders, disturbed by the rapidly increasing instances of extraterrestrial contact—some good, some bad—which enlists several scientific geniuses to create a plan to rid the universe of other life forms. The committee, spurred by the fear-mongering of the president of the United States of America (Jason Robards), places its faith in the hands of a brilliant, young, beautiful (of course) scientist (Angelina Jolie) who devises a plan to send manned super-nuclear warheads into outer space, to then be piloted toward each known planet in the solar system. This comprises roughly ten minutes of the film. The resulting three hours and twenty-five minutes are devoted to the actual suicide missions of the eight missiles, which are piloted by Toni Collette, Jude Law, Jada Pinkett-Smith, Tom Cruise, Matt Damon, Laurence Fishburne, Zhang Ziyi, and Robert Duvall. The star power at play is staggering, perhaps intentionally designed so as to allow the characters to withstand the awe-inspiring, divine setting of the film—some of it actually filmed in space. It should not ruin the movie to state that almost all of the participants in this mission are unsuccessful and it should not ruin the movie to say that the movie spends most of its time focusing on Collette, who is tasked with eliminating Pluto from the galaxy. Plot and character are, truthfully, not the interest of Beauregard; he cares, instead, about themes and visuals. The problem is that the plot and characters are presented in such a strange way that the film seems to actively work against the tenets of storytelling.

The greatest example has to be the way in which these world-famous actors are presented. For nearly the entirety of the film, these astronauts/suicide bombers don't wear helmets, which would obscure their faces, but, strangely enough, are encased in an oxygen-manufacturing cloud that protects their bodies from the stress of long-term space travel. This cloud is digitally created and works in the same way that offensive images are blurred on television, though in a more detailed, more ghost-like way. The actors seem not to be present, to instead already be perished and brought back to the film in ghost form. While the voices of these characters—and particularly unique voices like Duvall and Collette fare better than Cruise or Damon—are present, their bodies, their faces, are obscured for the duration of the film. Why, I ask, spend millions upon millions of dollars on actors who will not be seen? And some actors, such as Ziyi in particular, are primarily interesting actors because of their looks, their movements, not their voices.

However, to pinpoint one aspect of this film as overspending seems ludicrous. And, if the voices of these actors are to be prized, it is again strange that so much of the movie, I would say 75 percent, is silent. These are characters on single-manned space flights and they behave as such, sitting in their cockpits, occasionally floating through the cramped quarters that are not given over to the immense payload that is the primary purpose of the trip. It is, I have to say, much like watching a movie where everyone has died, including the director, and the film was reassembled in heaven and beamed back to Earth. It is, yes, unsettling and difficult.

The visuals are stunning. It is impossible, most of the time, to understand what we are witnessing, what is real and what is effect and what is actually a hallucination of our own creation. If it is possible, Beauregard shows us not the light of dying stars but the reincarnation of the stars into something brighter, more startling, more real. It is not enough to say that the visuals, objects moving through a vast expanse of space that cannot simply be understood by the human eye, make you believe in the existence of a god. It causes you to believe that Naylon Beauregard is a god, and this causes you to wonder why a god would create such a strange and unsettling film. There is a scene that many will reference, if they make it this far, where Collette's rocket speeds toward Pluto and Beauregard presents the exterior of the rocket, the size of a fingernail, in a dense and empty expanse of outer space. The scene continues, without sound, for twenty-seven minutes. It is possible, for three or four minutes at a time, to lose sight of the ship entirely, to forget what it is you are even staring at, that you are even watching a movie. You keep reminding yourself that this is a studio-backed summer blockbuster sci-fi adventure, but you are weeping and you cannot understand why we exist when we hold the capacity to hurt everything we've ever loved.

Though it is rarely done, it is necessary to discuss the ending. You are free to stop reading, but it won't matter. It won't prevent the necessary readjustment of your mind and body. Knowing in advance cannot prepare you for the sheer spectacle of watching an entire planet explode and vaporize. Other articles will discuss the audacity of a film crew searching for, discovering, and then blowing up an actual, honest-to-god planet (though even that designation is, apparently, still being debated, though without the actual planet to help aid in the discourse). The aim of this review is to simply state that the ending, the successful delivery of Collette's rocket into a planet, which then shifts to the actual footage that Beauregard painstakingly captured (using equipment and techniques he literally invented), is impossible to accurately describe. Even in the strangeness of the scene, having never witnessed an event like this before, it is perfectly understandable upon viewing it. You immediately understand that an object that took millions and millions of years to come into being has been destroyed. And you realize that it is not entirely dissimilar from the object that you currently inhabit.

The problem with reviewing *Essential Target* is that it is impossible to accurately classify it as a film. It is something else entirely, and that is perhaps why this review asserts the failure of the endeavor. It is not a movie. It is a universal experience, accidentally captured by a camera. It is our collective belief that we are both everything and nothing. I wish I never, ever, saw it.

LUCY CORIN

BABY ALIVE

Directed by Jake Kasdan. Starring: Sissy Spacek and John Stamos.

DETECTIVE WENDY BUCKEM (SISSY Spacek) finds herself on the trail of a killer targeting young mothers-to-be. Part thriller, part reality TV, the cast features MTV *Teen Mom* and *16 and Pregnant* reality stars (Catelynn, Farrah, Amber, Maci, Leah, Emily, Ebony, and Whitney). The young women struggle with their relationships, dreams, and new responsibilities while attempting to evade a mysterious stalker. As time runs out and bodies pile up, Detective Buckem finds herself confronting her own past. Also starring John Stamos.

Reviews:

★ ★ ★ ★ ★

Baby Alive sucks you in and never lets you go. If you want action with raw emotion and the added bonus of REAL people that lends an air of ambiguity, this movie will intrigue and inspire.

★ ★ ★ ★

I saw this movie in pre-release and found disjointed the attempt to merge so-called "reality" with actual celebrity within the same medium. Still, the plot itself is both familiar and functional, structured as a series of vignettes (or "episodes") in which we meet each teen mother before, during, or after her pregnancy, such that, prior to each demise, earlier mothers are making the decision to have unprotected sex with their boyfriends (or sometimes acquaintances or assailants), and later scenes show the young ladies increasingly pregnant, and so on. Thereby, an interesting effect occurs with respect to time, which I could get into further though not in this format. Some of the most affecting portrayals are actually the minor characters—the teen's family members, friends, and so on—who subtly look askance at the proceedings, and are in various ways positioned by force or happenstance to observe, as well, the killings, but then disappear from the film—not to get too deep, but perhaps like in life itself? In any case, the actors who play these minor characters are sometimes diamonds in the rough. Overall, the film merits a 3.5 but, as that option is not available, I give it 4 with the benefit of doubt.

★ ★ ★ ★ ★

The movie, enjoyable as it was, left me with many lingering questions. It doesn't say what he wants with the babies, even though there are only a few near the end. I know that some of the fathers we're supposed to think are good father figures, so maybe the babies left over go with him, but maybe there's a sequel about the real dads? I found that aspect confusing. Otherwise, this movie is good and I was engaged about our society at large as well as the internal lives of the people. I know people curse a lot in real life, but I also feel that you didn't need to have that many curse words to make your point.

★ ★ ★ ★ ★

Go Catelynn! I knew her in high school and she was never all that, but you gotta respect that she made more of her life than I did, ha!

★ ★ ★

How did they get Sissy Spacek to do this movie? Sissy Spacek of *Coal Miner's Daughter* and *Carrie* and *Badlands*? She is a class act; she must be having money problems? I saw her last year at a farmer's market in Virginia buying a bottle of olive oil for like twenty bucks so I don't get it at all. I liked the movie, though it wasn't worth the price of a ticket.

★ ★ ★ ★

I am very selective when it comes to giving a five-star rating, but this movie was awesome and it would have got five stars if it wasn't for the repetition in the methods the killer used. I know serial killers have to do it in the same way because they are compelled, but I also feel like swords are a little overdone and the director could have mixed it up a bit more. Other than that, it was fantastic viewing. John Stamos as the son/villain lends an air of brooding sophistication to the young cast.

★

This movie arrived cracked and when you kindly replaced it with another one, I was unable to turn off the dubbing, which was Chinese or something, making for an infuriating experience. You should have a way to rate it zero stars.

★ ★ ★ ★

Besides being genuinely suspenseful, this film has many themes and issues that it portrays. I enjoyed the symbol of the pacifier, or "nubbin," as it pertained to the serial killing/cutting body parts off aspects of the film. In terms of society at large, many of us have felt this way, and it lends a sense of reality to the relatable nature of the main character. There are some good comebacks in it and surprise twists. When I go to the movies, I don't need it to be Academy Award worthy; however, you should at least know how to act, so I have to admit some of the teen moms did seem scared. I was also appreciative of the production value, which is one thing that always kept me from enjoying the television version and reality TV in general.

★ ★ ★

Perhaps this movie was meant to be a satire, but someone in marketing didn't think that would sell? I heard that the original trailer featured the classic song "Baby Got Back" which is hysterical, but someone nixed it or got offended which is why they switched to serious.

★

I had that doll as a kid and was expecting a movie inspired by it, but if that's the case for you, you will be surely disappointed in this travesty of a movie. What we really want is to be entertained, instead you get something totally unexpected. You may remember *Baby Alive* as big compared to the usual dolls and pretty realistic. It came with a baby food assemblage and poop. You know *Transformers* is from toys right? I bet half of you don't even know you just want to bang Megan Fox—who doesn't? It's one thing for an artist to be inspired but it's another thing to rip something off and not even know it. I know it's geeky but I got a lot of education about life from that doll.

★ ★ ★ ★ ★

This film seems like it's all about the gore of the killer, but in the end it does have an uplifting message about the value of each and every child. I'm not saying it's the greatest movie ever, but my date and I both enjoyed it.

I am a teen mom and my own mother was murdered when my child was two months old. I'm sorry if that is TMI but only recently have I decided to try to watch movies because it's hard to find one that isn't triggering. So I think people should consider that. I saw this movie in the theater which was the first time I had been in a movie theater in I don't know how long. It was in a falling apart old school one downtown that is practically out of business but keeps hanging on. I don't remember much about the movie all I can say is I was glad I went, it was a big step for me in my life. Maybe someday I will be desensitized enough for a fuller appreciation.

★ ★ ★ ★

First off this movie is not about the Baby Alive Doll, it's about twelve reality star teen moms that SPOILER ALERT get knocked off one by one in the grand tradition of this type of movie, where the black guy either died first or by the end of the eighties he died second to last by saving everyone by selfless sacrificing his life, underlining a mirror of racism. The moms are actually pretty inspiring when you consider how hard it is to raise a baby in this day and age. I kind of knew about halfway through who the killer was, but I've seen a lot of movies like this and usually I know by the end of the credits so that's pretty good. There is also, for your information, a mechanical French duck from steampunk time that I saw in a museum that does the same thing as the doll with digesting etc. There's also a poem.

★ ★ ★ ★ ★

I remember that doll my friend had it! Gross! Also the teen moms need to get a life! But now they're dead!

STEPHEN GRAHAM JONES

THE BOY WHO CRIED ABOUT WOLVES

*Directed by Tim Sullivan. Starring: Ethan Landry,
Billy Wirth, Gwendolyn X, and Joe Don Baker.*

THIS IS NOT A call for censorship. So, if you've found this review through some outlet arguing for tighter controls on content, from watch groups promoting what they call "decency," or via some spokesperson decrying the moral decline contemporary cinema's contributing to, then please understand that that's not where my campaign dollars go. Loyal readers will of course know the opposite to be more the case, yes? Am I not the guy who said Rob Zombie's remake of Herschell Gordon Lewis's *Blood Feast* didn't go far enough? Did I not claim *Nudist Colony Massacre IV* was the true inheritor of Ingmar Bergman's body of work? Have I not circulated my *Cannibal Holocaust* remake petition enough for you to know my tastes? Is this column not called "Video Nasties"?

Still. Come on, people.

Ever since lycanthropy went legit, as they say—or came out of the closet or started baying at the moon or clawing at the door or whining at the foot of the bed or pick-your-euphemism—the parade of transformation sequences we've been subjected to has been almost comical, wouldn't you say? How many ways can human skin bubble and burst?

And it's not that I don't understand. Used to be, even a subpar transformation sequence would take a day to shoot and cost as much as a used Honda Accord. Now that you can hire somebody to do it on-camera for a couple of cheeseburgers and the promise of work next week, though, all our drama and sitcoms have jumped on the werewolf bandwagon. And the box office—please.

The Girl Who Screamed Wolf has got to be the twentieth movie with that title in the last two years. The only reason it even popped on my radar at all is Gwendolyn X, everybody's favorite maven, one of the few working actors whose tats are real, who can work a

Kickstarter if she needs to, and who brings her own MPAA rating in with her.

Granted, she doesn't always make the best decisions script-wise, but I'm not going to begrudge somebody for working, for pulling a check.

As for who she's playing opposite this time, well, if his name mattered, I'd put it in parentheses (here). He's a werewolf, that's all that matters. Tall dude, clear blue eyes, can't seem to keep a shirt on his chest. Before werewolves became a protected species, so to speak, he probably couldn't find work at the carwash. Now his dressing room, is the same size as the scream queen from *Diva Slumberparty Blues*.

And, this *The Girl Who Screamed Wolf*—remember when that variation on title carried with it the parable? When flipping the 'he' to 'she' even suggested a bit of the Cassandra myth, maybe even revealed our own cultural biases?

The studio doesn't either.

Put a 'she' in the title in Hollywood, and the audience expects either eighty-eight minutes of damsel-in-distress or an escalating series of unlikely wet T-shirt contests.

The Girl Who Screamed Wolf tries for both at once. Which can work, don't get me wrong. A shelf for everything and everything on its shelf, as they say.

But there comes a time. There comes a limit. Even for this boy.

First, the title doesn't come close to applying. The "girl" crying wolf in the trailer we all saw, it's not even Gwendolyn X's character Tanya Bateson. It's the neighbor girl, over in the first ten minutes to borrow a box of jello mix. Remember her standing at the door, calling back to Tanya that there's something out there, miss?

Don't feel bad. Five minutes after delivering her line, I'd forgotten her too. Leaving Tanya Bateson. And *The Girl Who Screamed Wolf*'s, ahem, "story?" Don't let me pull the rug out from under you here, but it's your typical low-budget home invasion kind of affair: Tanya Bateson is cat-sitting at a friend's house, and, because her friend told her it would look good on her, she uses her friend's hair dye, becoming platinum blond in the first sequence. This turns out to be a bad idea, as now she looks just like her friend, whose dangerous ex-boyfriend just got out of prison and is supposed to be lurking around, thus the friend's hasty exit.

You can see where this is going, yes? A handsome stranger at the door, Tanya Bateson unaccountably wearing a red-hooded cloak of all things, things escalating in the usual direction for a Gwendolyn X outing: steaming it up in the shower, the music dialed loud enough she can't quite hear the claws on the window, various contrived reflections of her trademark silhouette.

Wash, rinse, repeat for eighty-eight minutes, yes.

What's wrong with this picture, though, what I want to call your attention to, is that, whereas the spectacle is supposed to be Gwendolyn X and her questionable clothing decisions—you know what you're getting with her—what actually gets all the camera time are the transformations.

Let me lay them out for you:

> There's one beside the breakfast nook on the side of the house, in the big window behind Tanya Bateson eating French toast with syrup (imagine lots of crosscutting, here).

> There's one on the roof, by the chimney, with—get this— the full moon as a backdrop.

> There's a partial one in the shed in the backyard, with the kids camping out in the backyard next door, of course telling campfire stories.

> There's one right by the mailbox, behind the completely unwitting late-night pizza delivery boy, who, as it turns out, was delivering himself.

There's either another one in the backyard or this is edited-out footage of the first backyard transformation; either way, there's a cat and an owl watching. (You can already see their eyes, can't you? never blinking?)

There's one in the eventual bedroom the story gets to, with Tanya Bateson tied to a chair so she has to watch.

Then there's the final one, that either gets the animal-rights up in arms or puts a lump of indignation in the ACLU's throat: this tall dark stranger taking a butcher knife to the stomach and then having to transform to save himself.

And, I'll trust you to guess whether Tanya Bateson's cat-owner friend is the stabber there, and whether she asked Tanya to house-sit as bait, so she could finally get even with her ex-boyfriend.

I'll also leave it to others whether that stabbing is latex and a collapsing blade or what the studios are trying to call a "practical effect," which is of course code for: if we stabbed him, where's the scar?

No, what I want you to focus on for just a bit, if you can look away from all the online transformation videos, is the presence of seven "dramatically necessary" transformation sequences in the very limited space of one feature film. Now, taking into account that each sequence (hair, claws, fangs, all that blood, the creaking, the screaming, that thing with the eyes) goes for a healthy eight minutes, that leaves us...what? Thirty minutes for story? Wait, wait, no: got to subtract those pesky end credits. Twenty-five minutes for character development and plot, for nuance and particularity, for buildup and resolution, for emotional engagement—for, yes, those things we used to kindasorta get for our feature film dollar.

I'm turning into one of those film reviewers, yes.

Remember when a solid werewolf film had one set piece transformation sequence? Not necessarily because that's all production could budget in, but because of the transformation sequence there needs to be a spike in the dramatic baseline, doesn't there? It needs to be visual proof that this is real, that this is something we can no longer deny. It needs to be a point past which the story can't go back, can't be the same as it was.

I'm talking *An American Werewolf in London*, yes. And, no, it doesn't matter even one little bit that it's turned out that particular transformation sequence was real, that they only faked like it was special effects. I'm talking about how it was used in the story. How that transformation was the aberration, the strange attractor if you will, around which the rest of the narrative now had to learn to spin.

In this latest *The Girl Who Screamed Wolf*, though, the transformation sequences, they aren't aberrant at all. Rather, they're the norm.

And, before you raise your hand, Pesky McGee, yes, there's precedent, from the pre-lycanthropy days—1941, *The Wolf Man*, when we were asked to thrill and gag at the spectacle of this "impossible" transformation, when we were asked to peek through our fingers at the transgression happening on-screen, at this unnatural mixing of man and animal, Doc Moreau.

Consider that less conditioning of the audience, though. Consider it more representative of our own nature.

In the same way we started fetishizing transformations as soon as special effects would allow them some semblance of the "real," so had we, nearly fifty years before, smuggled the camera into the bedroom before even taking its price tag off.

I'm talking our own pornographic tendencies, people. And not the "uncovering the hidden"-impulse we all probably understand at some level, and possibly champion in certain environments, but the basic narrative structure.

Let me define for a moment: pornography is a story where the "boring parts" are the flimsy excuses that deliver us to the next set piece, that next—yes—money shot. A visual of that narrative form is the snake who just ate the Seven Dwarves: lump, flat part; lump, flat part; lump, flat part. And we usually fast-forward across those flat parts, yes? Why? Because they don't matter. Because they're not what we're there for. We want the lumps, the bulges, the protuberances.

But those narrative lumps, those dramatic spikes, those choreographed, in-the-contract set piece money shots, they're not always sex, people. We need to all understand that "pornography" is a format, not the content. There's hunting pornography, there's real-estate pornography, there's cooking pornography: whatever gets us to that next delectable dish, well, it's good enough, right? So long as we do definitely get that dish, and in the highest resolution possible.

This is how the transformation sequence is being used now, werewolf fans. The stories are no longer pitched as human dramas that escalate and deepen and get recharged when combined with lycanthropy. The stories are no longer dealing with the savage tendencies inherent to this human condition. Now werewolf stories, they're pitched as: we can do one transformation in the kitchen, and one beside the house—the lighting's good there—and one in the backyard, and one on the roof if we do it fast, and can we work my cat in somewhere?

And then when the movie clocks in at animated-feature length—oops—you split one of those transformation sequences in two, get up near that all-important hour-and-a-half mark.

It's an insult to the fans. It's an insult to me.

You know what I want to see? Not a return to pre-lycanthropy times—you can't go back, and I don't harbor shifters any ill will— but what I want is a werewolf movie that harkens back to when transformation was too expensive, meaning off-camera was the default setting. We used to laugh at a character stepping behind a tree in desperation, and some sad-sack German shepherd trotting out the other side as a scary "wolf," didn't we?

But, as cheesy as that was, what it left room for was story. For surprise and reversal, for sacrifice and painful decisions. Bubbling skin is great, don't get me wrong. Skin where we have to imagine the bubbling, though—it turns out that wasn't so bad either.

I could even stomach those four-foot "wolves" of yesterday, if I had to. I mean, now that what werewolves really look like and what they can do is out in the open—wouldn't it be nice to check back into the fantasy for a couple of hours? Which, maybe that's really the issue, after all. We go to the movies not for the real, but for the fake that feels real. Granted, right now we're locked in a cycle of addiction to the all-too-real, to transformation sequence after transformation sequence, like there's any real variation from one to the next, but I have faith, people. Not in the filmmakers, but in you, the audience. Once we stop giving our dollars to all *The Girl Who Screamed Wolf*s out there, the studios and distributors will have to adapt, will have to—get this—transform before our very eyes, into some new and unguessed-at creature.

Maybe even into a real storytelling industry.

That's a transformation I'd watch over and over.

BRIAN EVENSON

THE TRIGGER

Directed by Fritz Lang. Written by Fritz Lang. Starring:
Frank Overton, Eunice Grayson, and Ross Tilton.

NEAR THE END OF his life, shortly after making *The Thousand Eyes of Dr. Mabuse* (1960) when he was beginning to go blind, Director Fritz Lang committed to one last project, which he both wrote and directed. It is referred to in some of his letters as "Angel of Death" and in others as "The Trigger." It is the latter title under which the Bundesarchiv files the footage.

That footage has been assembled now by Lang specialist Julio Sternhagen, and will be shown later this week for the first time at Film Forum. Sternhagen offers a rough cut of the available footage, around eighty-five minutes.

The Trigger is concerned with the early sixties paranoia about nuclear destruction, as expressed in films like Lumet's *Fail-Safe* (1964) and Kubrick's *Doctor Strangelove* (1964). In it, actor Frank Overton plays a once prominent but now neglected film director named Jacob Lahn. Lahn has been approached to direct a B movie about the nuclear destruction of Los Angeles. At first, Lahn is reluctant to take on the project, feeling it to be an artistic compromise, but his wife, played by Eunice Grayson (of James Bond fame), convinces him that they need the money. Reluctantly, Lahn accepts.

And then he reads the script closely and something changes for him: he begins to see what he might do with it. His bearing changes, his gaze becomes glassy, more distant, though with the film's expressionist camera work it takes a while for the viewer to notice this. As the planning progresses, Lahn begins to become increasingly serious about the project, even obsessed with it. He demands a closed set, letting actors only see part of the project and discussing only their individual scenes with them. He fires the head actor playing the man who hijacks a nuclear warhead and replaces him with an unknown actor named Ross Tilton (this being both the name of the character playing an actor within the film and the actor's actual name).

Tilton follows Lahn around like a puppy dog, adoringly, and quickly we begin to understand that his relation to Lahn is more like the relationship of a cult member to a cult leader than a movie actor to his director.

At this point there is a lacuna in the film, a series of scenes that Lang never managed to shoot. A single title screen appears, reading, "According to the script, things are further arranged and Lahn manages to fool the producer to give him a great deal of money. He will use this to pay someone to steal an actual warhead."

When the film resumes, the cinematography has changed. It is still expressionist, but the film stock is grainy and dim and smoky, the figures very difficult to see. Overton still plays Lahn, but the actor playing Tilton might well have changed—either that or his makeup has been done quite differently. Whereas before we had honest and open close-ups, we now have almost nothing but long shots, the camera angles more voyeuristic and hidden. Formal dialogue has been replaced by bits and snippets of things overheard. We follow Lahn and Tilton around, and slowly gather, or think we gather, hints that they are up to no good. Lahn tells Tilton he is planning to shoot the movie to its penultimate scene and then the two of them will retreat to safety, detonate the bomb, and film the final scene. It will destroy Hollywood, perhaps make much of Los Angeles uninhabitable, but, Lahn insists, it will be better this way. Tilton is enough of an adoring acolyte by now that he seems to simply accept this.

We keep expecting a hero to break in on the scene and wrest control away from Lahn, or Tilton to realize how he has been brainwashed, or Lahn to come to his senses. But none of this happens. Instead, according to Sternhagen's program notes, Lang dismissed most of the crew and filmed the rest of the film himself. With Lang going blind, the camera work is erratic and irregular, the lighting going through strange shifts, but it is no less effective for being so. It is as if we have entered the mind of a madman. There is a decided change in the acting on the part of Lahn and Tilton, a weird hesitancy as if they no longer know how seriously to take their roles, and they begin to avoid the prop of the warhead as if worried that it may, perhaps, be real.

We follow Lahn and Tilton in their plans. Having finished the shooting, Lahn grabs Tilton and leaves the set with him, telling the other actors that they need to consult and they'll be back in a moment. They drive some distance away, high into the Hollywood Hills. "Is this far enough away that we'll be safe?" asks Tilton of Lahn, and Lahn shrugs, then looks straight at the camera. Here ends the footage we have of the film.

Sternhagen speculates: "Why did Lang stop here? In the end did he decide not to pull the trigger? Did he disavow the film but find himself unwilling to destroy it? Or did he simply run out of money and was waiting to shoot the missing middle section and the final scenes?"

It is hard to say. As a film about obsession, about someone working to turn art into life (or more rightly death), *The Trigger* has much to recommend it. The acting is not as strong as it could be and the plot is far from perfect, but there is, as with even the most flawed of Lang's movies, something there, something that refuses to be dismissed.

STEFAN KIESBYE

BURNED

Directed by Michael Mann. Starring: Kenneth Branagh, Stanley Tucci, Kris Kristofferson, Corinna Harfouch, Ewan McGregor, Judy Dench, Til Schweiger, Jürgen Prochnow, and Carey Mulligan.

I SAW THIS MOVIE at the Berlin Film Festival in February, on a dreary night, when new snow settled on the old in such rapid manner that even hard-faced and dead-eyed Berliners stopped in their tracks to marvel at the sheer volume of the white, or at least near-white, mess dumped on their streets. Water accumulated in my sensible shoes.

The theater was overheated, for which I was grateful, and smelled of wet socks, for which I was not. The projector failed already during opening credits, and we waited in near darkness for over twenty minutes for the show to resume.

I'm not sure what Hollywood's fascination with Berlin is— and has any other city save Moscow endured more at the hands of America's filmmakers? The shots of decaying facades, the obligatory filters that turn every bit of natural color into a steely gray, or a steely blue—Berlin, even twenty years after the fall of the Wall, still looks more Kafka than capital, if Kafka had written third-rate spy novels. Enter Michael Mann and his movie *Burned*, which was shot on location throughout. Mann, in whose hands even Miami can seem like something Sarah Palin might use for Caribou-hunting, has outdone his predecessors and invented a new shade for this vast city. It's what can only be called a steely brown and it goes a long way to show us just how dangerous the German capital is.

The crowd didn't seem to mind that color. When the Brandenburg Gate, the symbol of the Cold War and of German reunification, appeared during the first thirty seconds of the movie, it was greeted with cheers. Beer bottles were raised every time a street sign or landmark appeared onscreen. In Berlin, it seems, people are grateful just to be noticed, even if only for the wrong things.

Hollywood's A-list actors have regularly descended on Berlin. From Tom Cruise to Liam Neeson to Matt Damon, they have scattered lovers and corpses in desolate streets, chintzy clubs, bars that haven't been cleaned since Hitler's regime, and hotel rooms where you don't have to look for bed bugs because they are already celebrating your arrival on the flower-patterned spread.

This time it's Kenneth Branagh who has to enter Berlin and look for dark secrets, secret identities, and operatives who may or may not be working for the people they say they're working for. We know that nobody is who they say they are and don't trust Stanley Tucci, the US Ambassador, who appears to be a decent guy but has a thing for underage Eastern prostitutes, and we don't even believe Kris Kristofferson, a former CIA operative who has stayed in the city that allowed him many decades of Cold War glory, when he grunts, "Of course it's the truth, I made it for you myself."

Branagh, as our hero Harry Trust, is a curious choice. He doesn't have the star power of many of Mann's previous collaborators, but he feels right in a way that no Robert De Niro or Tom Cruise ever has. In his younger years, Branagh often seemed overeager and nervous, preferring the grand gestures of the stage to the near non-acting the big screen requires. But he has settled comfortably into his once lithe body, his face has filled out and gained gravitas, and he moves with the knowledge that life is full of traps and that most big successes are only the preludes to even bigger failures. I liked his work in the Kurt Wallander TV movies on PBS, and here he gave his finest performance yet. He's nuanced, weighed down by too much experience, yet not defeated. He's on this mission only because his superiors want him gone without having to fire him, but he refuses to acknowledge that. He knows that spies can come back from the dead.

A woman he once had an affair with has been murdered. When he visits the morgue he doesn't recognize her immediately. She has aged, just like Harry, and his memories don't track. It's a memorable shot, Harry tracing the lines of German actress Corinna Harfouch who is a star in her country but is not allowed the tiniest wink or smirk.

That woman, once code-named Red Pigeon, was believed to be a useful double agent, betraying secrets to Moscow her American handlers knew to be false. After the end of the Cold War many thought her to slide into irrelevance, but Harry insists that she must have known something that made her death necessary. Of course, he's right.

In many ways, Michael Mann has never been an original filmmaker. His stories have been told twice and thrice and often many times more, yet I haven't missed any of his offerings yet. There's a quietness in even the loudest of his productions, an eerie sense that all the mayhem is happening to people who—just like those dead-eyed Berliners—would rather stop and stare at the mounds of snow just as they're being buried by them.

And I, for one, am glad to stare with them. *Miami Vice* was not about Sonny Crockett blowing up scores of baddies, and *The Last of the Mohicans* did not revel in bloody rituals. Instead, watching Daniel Day-Lewis hunt deer in buckskin, noiselessly, effortlessly is a revelation. In *Collateral*, even the parlor trick of giving Tom Cruise a gray head of hair is a touch of brilliance.

Mann's movies' outcomes are never in doubt. He is the rare filmmaker who seems to forget the story while he is making it. In this, he is a direct descendant of Don Siegel, the B-movie auteur who found his freedom and virtuosity in the run-of-the-mill sixty-minute flick. In *Heat*, we never believe that Robert De Niro could escape into retirement. In *Collateral*, we know that Tom Cruise cannot go unpunished. And so it is in *Burned*, too. Harry will win, and he will lose it all, and Mann never stoops to bore us with unnecessary plot twists.

Harry, who can't trust anyone, stumbles through Berlin and its steely brown autumn. Of course, Red Pigeon was onto something (I won't spoil the fun, but it involves Middle Eastern rogues). Of course, Harry gets beaten often and badly, and of course Stanley Tucci is so deeply involved in her death that "double agent" seems too quaint a term to describe him. And still I watched in awe, even forgetting my wet socks.

British actors, it must be said, seem to make the most reliable movie Germans. I was waiting for Gary Oldman to jump out at me with some showy throat-clearing consonants Hollywood imagines to sound German. Instead it was Ewan McGregor, reprising his role in *The Ghost Writer*, as an author steeped in espionage and with a brutally shortened life, who tries himself at appearing Teutonic. Judy Dench, in a cameo even shorter than Kristofferson's, is equally convincing at sounding, if not German, then strangely *foreign*.

The German actors who make appearances are another matter. Til Schweiger, who had a forgettable and silent role in Hollywood's *Replacement Killers*, and could recently be seen as a quiet killer in Quentin Tarantino's *Inglorious Basterds,* is not allowed a single sentence. He is offed quickly by a reluctant yet efficient Harry. Jürgen Prochnow, still known stateside as the doomed captain of *Das Boot*, plays an old Nazi, who assumed a false identity and tended gardens for fifty years and is now brought to trial. Soon I was waiting for some well-known German actor or actress to play a cyborg; alas, not even Middle Eastern rogues employ cyborgs in these cash-strapped times. However, all Middle Eastern rogues, as far as I could tell, were played by Germans.

As Harry runs from, and dispenses with, unshaven baddies —which, it must be noted, are never as bad or as effective, let alone intelligent, as a cleanly shaven Stanley Tucci, thus making a convincing case against facial hair—he picks up a damsel in distress (a subdued and utterly convincing Carey Mulligan). She is, of course, not in distress, but out to make Harry's life hell on earth, until she falls for our hero. We know how such things end from *Casino Royale*, but a dying Carey Mulligan, signaling to Harry her undying love, still produced countless sobs in the crowd.

So convincing is Michael Mann's vision of Berlin, that, when I finally left the theater and hurried through ice, snow, and slosh to the nearest subway entrance, I wished for some more brown shades. The reality of snowed-in Berlin was a touch brutal after watching *Burned*, the city streets less convincing than what I had just watched on the silver screen. Steely brown had made it almost believable. Bearable too.

JULIA INGALLS

WERNER HERZOG ON MICHAEL JACKSON: HE'S BAD?

Directed by Werner Herzog. Featuring interviews with Quincy Jones, Janet Jackson, and Pat Buchanan.

WERNER HERZOG HAS MADE a career out of celebrating madness. He doesn't glorify it or condone it; rather, he Teutonically whips back the curtain and cranks the footlights. It's up to you to decide whether you're revolted, fascinated, or unexpectedly moved. His decision to make a documentary about the life and death of pop star Michael Jackson is, in many ways, his natural artistic throughline: here, Herzog explores not just the madness of one individual, but of an entire culture. This is Herzog's *King Lear*.

"Whether he was a pedophile swaddled in the suffocating robes of celebrity culture," Herzog monologues over footage of Jackson playing with his monkey Bubbles, "or an abused boy-child whose socially internalized self-hatred made him an easy target for opportunists, Jackson was not a pop star but rather the embodiment of American tragedy. With his single white glove and increasingly bizarre surgical adventures, Jackson was both the guiding light and the sleazy underbelly of Reagan-era America."

Herzog is not focused on Jackson's guilt or innocence as a child molester, but rather the simple reality of his stardom in a country that was constantly pivoting between the poles of overheated religious rhetoric and velociraptor-like consumerism. Herzog essentially asks: What person does such a society choose as its figurehead? *He's Bad*, therefore, is neither a biopic, straight-up documentary, or Errol Morris-style cultural critique. By featuring the usual Herzogian detours, it becomes a delicious combination of all three. Instead of the coda of the albino alligators in *Cave of Forgotten Dreams*, Herzog swings into late-1980s Florida, where Republican strategist Lee Atwater is mastering his aggressive push-polling tactics.

"Among the sunny citrus groves and treacherous everglades, we find Atwater combining racial invective, sexual hate politics, and religious extremism to create a threshing machine for rational thought and debate. Atwater's needless destruction of the United States' democratic process in a time of relative national prosperity mirrors the gradual self-mutilation and bizarre personal behavior of multimillionaire Michael Jackson."

Herzog overlays this monologue on an increasingly powerful intercut between "Bille Jean," 1980s news footage, and still photos of garish, overpriced items from Jackson's home. As the sidewalk panels light up under Jackson's feet, we begin to feel that we are witnessing a gorgeously choreographed sequence of destruction. It's not just Jackson who is walking on surreal ground; he is simply the sequin-laden stand-in for an entire society.

The fact that Werner Herzog now lives in the US but is also inherently an outsider to the culture humanizes his portrait of Jackson. Instead of portraying him as a freak or punchline, Herzog sees Jackson as a man caught in vicious, puzzling circumstances. Much like his portrait of Timothy Treadwell in *Grizzly Man*, this is not a voyeuristic snark-tour, but rather a heartfelt examination of the inherently unanswerable question: Why?

Whatever your personal feelings about Jackson, it's difficult not to feel moved by the silent montage of Jackson and the women in his life. We watch as he sits with Elizabeth Taylor at a dinner party, meets with his eventual look-alike Diana Ross, and wince-inducingly kisses Lisa Marie Presley onstage. In the absence of sound, we see an alienated man doing his best to connect with his idealized version of love, and failing. It's fitting, therefore, that the final scene in the movie is taken from one of Michael Jackson's first appearances on television. Again, Herzog nixes the original interview soundtrack in favor of his voiceover as we watch a seemingly healthy, happy young boy speak into an interviewer's microphone.

"Perhaps the best way to remain unknown is to become world-famous," Herzog laments. "In this way, Michael Jackson succeeded. In all others, he failed."

ROY KESEY

ABBOTT AWAITS

*Directed by Paul Thomas Anderson from the novel by
Chris Bachelder.*

THERE ARE SO VERY many ways for bad movies to come of good books, and so many of those ways have to do with distance: that is, with directors too insecure to stretch away from the text even when the new medium demands it, or too daft to realize they have wandered off the text's most essential paths. Making a great movie from a great book, on the other hand, requires an unbroken chain of small miracles—which is why so few such things exist. And yet and yet and yet: here now before us is Paul Thomas Anderson's magnificent adaptation of the timeless Chris Bachelder novel *Abbott Awaits*.

The book itself was published to widespread critical acclaim; in the words of *TNYRB* literary critic Mateo Campana, "There is in this world only one marriage, and all of us live it, and this novel is its definitive account." Sam Lipsyte called it "a sly and soaring novel about fear and tenderness and family," and Keith Lee Morris alleged Bachelder to have invented an entirely new genre known as "Existential Domestic Cosmology." It is perhaps a surprise that a director best known for his hyperkinetic camerawork and large ensemble casts should have chosen this seemingly small, quiet project—particularly now, when wisehearted looks at marriage seem most often relegated to the small screen, whether as drama (think Kyle Chandler and Connie Britton as Eric and Tami Taylor on *Friday Night Lights*) or as comedy (say, Ty Burrell and Julie Bowen as Phil and Claire Dunphy on *Modern Family*.) But as it turns out, Existential Domestic Cosmology is a genre in which Anderson feels entirely at home.

The central casting dilemma for *Abbott Awaits* was neatly solved by turning to the most consistently brilliant member of Anderson's informal rep company: Philip Seymour Hoffman. Hoffman's many-shaded silences and unusually animated expressions (he reportedly lost forty pounds for the jowl-less role) allow Anderson to sidestep the distasteful consequences, all too common in adaptations, of excessive (i.e., any) reliance on voice-over. Riskier was Anderson's decision to cast Maya Rudolph—his real-life life partner and the mother of his four children—as Abbott's wife. Rudolph steers clear of *SNL*-style mugging and *Bridesmaids* pratfalls, coming through splendidly as an intelligent, conflicted, complicated woman searching for her share of grace. The cast is rounded out by the usual subjects acquitting themselves well in smaller-than-usual parts. We have Philip Baker Hall as a creepily intense pet store owner, and John C. Reilly as an obtuse but well-meaning neighbor; Melora Walters and Michael Penn as scientists researching fireflies, and Luis Guzmán as a refrigerator repairman; Ricky Jay as chief of staff at the butterfly conservatory, a spry and clean-shaven Burt Reynolds as a plumber, Julianne Moore as an obstetrician, and Alfred Molina as an unforgettable anesthesiologist.

The film's scenes tend to run shorter than Anderson usually works, but his infamously long tracking shots function perfectly as a form of directorial patience: they allow him to explore nook after cranny in the life of Abbott, a university professor off work for the summer and thus home for the last three months of his insomniac wife's pregnancy with their second child. Abbott spends much of his time cleaning up after their toddler daughter, scrubbing ancient raisins off of high chairs and raspberry vomitus out of car seats. He wrestles rolls of cat-sprayed carpet out to the curb, succeeds as often as he fails in attempts to deal with household emergencies, and spends his scarce free moments on the Internet looking up obscure trivia, diagnosing himself with diseases he does not actually have, and forcing himself to confront the suffering of others: he clicks on link after link, finding his way to photographs of children disfigured by Chernobyl, to footage of what appears to be a weeping fetus, to interviews held with the families of trapped miners, all so as to incline himself (sincerely if artificially) toward the gratefulness he knows he should feel for the life he has.

Hoffman's acting chops are well up to the task of endowing Abbott's many internal paradoxes ("Abbott is not a prude about porn. Or, to put it another way, he is a prude about porn." / "Abbott would like to think he's a *good guy*, and yet his wife is up there sobbing, and he's down here with the superglue." / "The following prepositions are both true: (A) Abbott would not, given the opportunity, change one significant element of his life, but (B) Abbott cannot stand his life." / "What kind of fool would cherish this? What kind of fool would not cherish this?") with precisely the clarity and humor and genuine affect found in the source material. This is not to say, of course, that Anderson never veers from the novel, but when he does, it is in wholly justifiable ways: the story makes as much sense in his beloved San Fernando Valley as it did in Bachelder's Western Massachusetts, and if you'll permit me the smallest of spoilers, the narrative is actually strengthened when Anderson, unlike Bachelder, allows Abbott and his wife to finally go ahead and buy the couch they've spent the whole movie searching for. (The fact that they buy it from a show-stealing William H. Macy makes the scene all the more satisfying.)

Nonetheless, the movie as a whole would likely have failed without strong work by Anderson's crew, particularly cinematographer Robert Elswit and set designer Conny Boettger. In perhaps the most notable example, a single silent take renders up every nuance of Bachelder's phrasing: following Abbott's painful fall on his way up the basement stairs, we see "[t]he shirts [...] strewn, as if they had grappled at the top and then tumbled down. Their backs look broken. A blue one has an arm outstretched, as if trying to break its fall, or to reach for something out of reach."

Abbott's constant search for evidence of human nobility, and his struggle to do both good and well within his wholly contemporary life, are in the end invested with as much import as the most transparently Herculean of endeavors. That is to say, he too spends most of his hours and days reaching for things out of reach. It is to this film's great credit that we never want him doing anything else.

ANTOINE WILSON

MINE

Directed by Guillame Abruzzo. Starring: Channing
Tatum, Tabu, and Rufus Sewell. With Max Perlich.

THE FIRST LINE OF dialogue in Guillame Abruzzo's ponderous but ultimately compelling science fiction film *Mine* is a single mumbled four-letter word for excrement. An unnamed astronaut (Max Perlich), attempting an arduous docking maneuver, has just botched the job, resulting in the implosion of the vehicle with which he's trying to dock, and the deaths of the several astronauts we've just seen sitting inside.

That Abruzzo's war-is-hell-in-space film opens with such a scene is not remarkable in and of itself. That it occurs eighteen minutes into *Mine* is astonishing. For a full eighteen minutes, without music or dialogue, we watch Perlich prepare for the docking. He checks his calculations, works on the computers, fidgets with a valve, all in silence. He's got no HAL or GERTY to talk to. His capsule is a dump, papered over with drawings and notes, random detritus floating past while he works.

In lesser hands, this would be about as exciting as watching a computer programmer at work. But Abruzzo guides our vision toward the astronaut's bloodshot eyes, his uneven stubble, the recurring itch in his left ear. We don't see what he's typing, but he hits the delete key more than seems normal. When the docking fails and the vehicle implodes, Abruzzo presents the abrupt shift from drudgery to tragedy as a fact of life, nothing else.

We see in Perlich's world-weary (space-weary?) eyes such a loss of hope that we know what's coming next before he does. Again, Abruzzo refuses to telegraph, sticking with a medium shot. The only thing in motion is the astronaut's arm, first crossing himself, then reaching for a lever that sucks everything out of the cabin, including him, leaving us to look at the cored-out hull of a ship, now merely space junk. Reading this, one might be tempted to interpret this as an act of hari-kari, a self-sacrifice in the face of dishonor. But after waiting eighteen minutes for it, the meaning is unmistakable: Perlich's astronaut can't bear to be alone for another moment.

By this point, half of the audience has likely filed out of the theater. This is not the movie they've been sold in the trailers. That movie does show up, eventually, with music, and dialogue, and scenes set on an Earth much like ours. There are no funky costumes, no futuristic cars. No alien invasion. Only advanced space-travel technology.

We are, as usual, at war with each other. The players are divided into three factions: a EuroAmerican Coalition, a PanAsian Group, and an Anonymous-like collective of privateers and hackers (called Kernel) operating out of a base near Birdling's Flat in New Zealand.

Space archaeologists (the identities of which are never made clear) have discovered a highly protected and booby-trapped burial-chamber-cum-mine on the Martian surface. After an attempt at a joint mission, the botched docking incident has prompted the EuroAmericans and PanAsians to declare war on each other in pursuit of whatever lies beneath the Martian surface. The Kernel team functions as a sort of terrorist third-party.

Abruzzo isn't one for battlefields or lasers shooting across the vastness of space. He prefers cameras mounted inside space helmets, fogging up with each breath. There are no buildings on Abruzzo's Mars—meaning nobody takes their helmets off outside the spaceships. Everyone is isolated within their own spacesuit and bubble-mask. Why, one might ask, hire Channing Tatum as your leading man if he's going to spend most of your movie behind a full-face version of mirrored sunglasses? (The answer probably lies in shooting schedules—Abruzzo is a notoriously slow director, and Tatum's character is played by a body double for much of the film.)

Once on Mars, the factions recognize that they must rely on each other to survive. The petty differences that separated them on Earth are momentarily put aside as they face the fact that the ancient civilization has done everything in its power to protect the loot from outsiders. Abruzzo seems neglectfully disdainful of this part of the film. There's speculation that the factions' sudden spirit of cooperation stemmed from a studio note, and that Abruzzo's killing off Tatum shockingly early was his response. In any case, Tatum's death sets off a series of fatal skirmishes, including hand-to-hand combat, in space suits, on the Martian surface. For a spell, Abruzzo loses himself in a Spielbergian playground of references, dropping nods to everything from *Three Kings* to Charlton Heston's little-known prospectors-and-propellers film *Mother Lode*.

In the end, two astronauts are left: the PanAsian group's Tabassum (played by the Indian actress Tabu) and Kernel's Haxxor (played by Rufus Sewell). Deep in the complex, at the final door blocking the way to the mine's inner chamber, Haxxor sabotages Tabassum's oxygen and she's forced to return to her ship. Haxxor, welding tools in hand, manages to penetrate the final chamber: the heart of the mine. Suddenly, a crackling sound dominates the soundtrack—Haxxor's Geiger counter—and he vomits inside his helmet, collapsing to the ground. The prize, it turns out, is an ancient nuclear waste storage container, the "booby traps" intended as a warning system, a benevolent KEEP OUT sign left behind by an ancient civilization.

Tabassum doesn't make it to her ship. Abruzzo gives us a long shot of Tabassum's suit, supine in the Martian dust, then cuts to a camera inside her helmet. Her eyes flutter. The final image is her view of the vastness of space; it flickers to black every time she blinks. This goes on for three and a half minutes. As the blinks grow longer, we notice—I'm not sure if some digital effects nudge us or if we naturally end up focusing on it—the tiny blue Earth among the stars and planets.

Mine is a narrative of pettiness, avarice, and bellicosity resulting in nothing. As such, it puts on grand display the worst of human nature. But within his plot, Abruzzo refuses to let go of the essential humanity of his characters; their nobler selves must contend with the roles they are fated to play. These forms have been around since the Ancient Greeks, but in Abruzzo's vision, there's a crucial difference: the gods have absconded. Civilization tends toward self-destruction, Abruzzo seems to be saying, and while the individuals comprising that civilization have no chance of escape, they do have the right to their own little pieces of subjectivity, if only for the time being.

MAILE CHAPMAN

DR. DISGRACE

Directed by David Cronenberg. Starring: Sandra Vergara, Abigail Breslin, Zendaya, Isis King, Robert Patrick, Daniel Dae Kim, Patti Hansen, Tommy Lee Jones, Sonia Manzano, Bryan Cranston, and Johnny Depp as Dr. Dipak Desai.

DR. DISGRACE BEGINS WITH a patient (Robert Patrick) heading home after—joy of all joys—a routine colonoscopy in a crowded clinic. "What about this?" he asks, tapping the bandage on his forearm. "Just take it off when you get home," he's told. He rides in a cab down streets lined with beige medical buildings and little stucco offices with signs in English and Spanish—lawyers, payday loans, bail bondsmen—before turning into a neighborhood of tidy ranch-style houses in grassless yards. Jagged red mountains ring the desert skyline; only as he unlocks the battered security door of his house do we see the iconic lights of the Las Vegas Strip in the distance. When the man pulls the tape from his arm, a red gout of blood saturates the rug at his feet and he finds an IV needle, left behind in his vein at the clinic.

So begins the film: glittering riches in the distance, the gorier realities of life firmly in the foreground.

If you're squeamish, stop here. If not, meet Dr. Dipak Desai (Johnny Depp). Depp's Desai is based on a once real-life physician, owner of several successful endoscopy clinics, and generous donor to the local Hindu temple of the same name. But when real-life Desai, who lived with his wife in a $3.4-million home in the Vegas Valley, began cutting corners to save money, his scrimping would eventually expose forty thousand—yes, *forty thousand*—patients to HIV, Hepatitis B, and Hepatitis C through tainted injections, unclean instruments, and the kind of carelessness that leaves needles behind in patients' bodies.

In director David Cronenberg's version of these now-public events, the whole disgraceful affair is parsed by a class of college students at the University of Nevada, Las Vegas, who devote a semester to sifting through the events at the clinic and the ensuing media attention under the guidance of their ethics professor (Sonia Manzano, in a role that will gladden the hearts of every forty-something who remembers her as Maria from *Sesame Street*). The cast includes Sandra Vergara, Abigail Breslin, Zendaya, and Isis King as an assortment of pretty young co-eds with lives that seem so easy, until we see that one has addiction issues, one is a teenage single mom, one is transgender, and one has, well, let's just say a bad boyfriend and a questionable side job. Tommy Lee Jones, an abrasive libertarian rancher who "doesn't believe the hype," joins the crew alongside Daniel Dae Kim, the quietly traumatized veteran who believes in conspiracies of silence. The group also includes Patti Hansen as a woman returning to finish her bachelors degree after her kids leave for college (mirroring her own return to the screen after a hiatus of nearly three decades), and an odd performance by Jaden Smith as a physics prodigy who appears bored during discussions about ethics. Together, the class absorbs the grisly details of the case, condemning Desai by degree without totally dismissing his humanity. (Which is not to say that Desai isn't an evil man; fans of Cronenberg who come to *Dr. Disgrace* expecting a film along the lines of *Dead Ringers* or *The Brood* may find this film disappointing... until the scenes of Desai gowning up and conducting procedures in his clinic.)

Some of what Cronenberg has Desai do is beyond ludicrous and yet terribly mundane, like making his staff cut disposable hygienic bed pads in half to save twenty cents, or skimping on basic cleaning supplies. Others are disturbingly meticulous, like hiring certified nurse anesthetists rather than anesthesiologists, a distinction that lets him (over)bill insurance companies and avoid the scrutiny of his medical peers. But these are nothing compared to his actions in the procedure room (more on that in a moment) and his inexcusable decision to reuse bottles of anesthesia intended for single use with a single patient. Desai deliberately violates the

drug maker's guidelines and routinely puts his patients at risk—and
when the bottles get low, he consolidates the contents, spreading
the risk as far as possible. (In real life, eight patients with acute Hep
C are known to have gotten it in Desai's clinic, and one of them
has since died; so far, over a hundred more have been identified,
including those infected indirectly.)

As the students come to realize, the bigger picture is
complicated by the question of drug company liability, the failure
of Desai's bullied staff to blow the whistle, and the degree to which
the HMO he worked for is responsible for the injuries he caused.
This last is a central question. His services were cheap, but were
they too cheap? He did more colonoscopies more quickly and
for less money, and there's no doubt that the HMO rewarded his
"efficiency," but did they know he was a rotten doctor and decide
to look the other way? This is the type of suspicion that haunts
the students, whose growing distrust of medical authority leads
them into increasingly bizarre forms of paranoia. One refuses to
immunize her baby; another stops taking anti-seizure medication,
preferring to risk brain damage than trust the student health
center staff. One who works nights at a hotel on the Strip gets fired
and then arrested for overreacting (and how) to a random drug
test, while another suffers insomnia to the point of violent sexual
hallucinations with all-too-real consequences. These ruptures
happen in addition to their other challenges; some are first-
generation college students, non-native speakers of English, all are
strapped for cash, and the economic crisis looms constantly in the
background like the glittering skyline of the casinos behind the
law school library where they meet each week.

Even so, it's really Depp's movie, though he never speaks.
Depp captures Desai's heavy face, the empty bloodshot eyes, and
the creepily aggressive silence; he radiates deep malevolence even
as his defense attorney tries to convince a judge that he isn't fit to

stand trial because of a series of jailhouse strokes (brought on, no doubt, by the strain of being held accountable). One doesn't want to be unkind to a man who isn't well—especially not during an exploration of ethics and the failure of professional empathy—but it's hard to see Desai as a fellow human being. Robert Eglet, legal counsel for the patients who sue the HMO (Bryan Cranston, in a pinstriped suit and heavy glasses), is the embodiment of contained moral outrage in the courtroom scenes. His summation—taken from transcripts—uses *monkey see, monkey do,* and *monkey say* to illustrate the secrecy, failure to act, and pressure to remain silent at the clinic (his graphics would be in terrible taste if the whole affair wasn't already so over the top).

Eglet is as sensational as he needs to be, describing Desai as the "fastest endoscopist in the west," what others in the field call a "jammer"—Desai was so fast, in fact, that he'd been known to splatter feces on the walls and ceilings when yanking his scope out of the viscera of his unconscious patients. (Knowing this, his refusal to give his staff enough disinfectant to properly clean the scopes of blood, tissue, and waste between procedures is all the more indecent.)

The students form their own conclusions, according to their political and religious beliefs; one prays for Desai, another wants to see him get the death penalty, and a third contemplates killing him with a high-powered rifle. By the end of the film, a jury finds the HMO liable for $24 million in damages, pharmaceutical companies are sued to the tune of $500 million, and Desai is charged with second-degree murder and other crimes.

But there's little satisfaction in any of this, especially when the attorneys gather their files and step aside, and we see, sitting in court, the patients who got sick. Almost all of the students in the group finish the semester knowing that convention alone is the fragile basis of public trust, and that our safety and peace of mind have always depended on the non-malevolence of strangers. In other words, don't expect a happy ending.

J. RYAN STRADAL

A BIRD IN THE HAND

Directed by Martin Brest. Screenplay: Eleven writers credited. Starring: Hugh Grant, Jennifer Aniston, Zooey Deschanel, Michael Cera, Julia Roberts, Queen Latifah, and Stanley Tucci.

ONCE EVERY DECADE OR SO, a film comes along that's so familiar, palliative, and obvious that merely focusing on it becomes an exercise in reining in the cultural associations it inspires in your subconscious. Days later—hours in some cases—it becomes difficult for viewers to remember anything about the film, and at best they are left with distinct emotional sensations akin to a prolonged experience of déjà vu.

The plot of *A Bird in the Hand* is easy enough to delineate, if you write it down while you're watching it: Doyle Southampton (Hugh Grant), a rakish British lawyer living in New York City, is about to settle down with his smart but high-maintenance girlfriend Jessica Bird (Jennifer Aniston), when Jessica's fun-loving, hipster younger sister Cambridge Bird (Zooey Deschanel), whose age difference is explained by Jessica calling her "the family accident," shows up from college and sweeps Doyle off his feet.

Reading this, you may ask how, if they've been dating for three years and living together, Doyle has never met his girlfriend's sister before, but this question doesn't occur to you while you're watching the film, because by the time Cambridge is introduced, your skills of perception and discernment are so thoroughly benumbed, someone could replace your popcorn with a bucket of tartar sauce and it'd be five minutes before you'd notice or care.

So, with a week before the wedding, Doyle must decide between the Bird sisters, contending with Cambridge's jealous "just a friend" boy-pal Jimmie (Michael Cera), his sassy, all-seeing law partner Monique (Queen Latifah), the fussy gay wedding planner (Stanley Tucci), and his childhood friend and confidante Molly (Julia Roberts). Yes, you've seen this all before, from the token sassy non-sexual black character, to the token fussy gay character, to the high-maintenance, put-upon modern woman, to the manic pixie dream girl, to the shy nerdy wallflower dude, to the hate-him-so-much-ya-love-him dissolute rake, to the patient and loyal secret crush. And more to the point, you've seen it just like this.

For six days, through the rehearsal dinner, pratfalls ensue as Doyle conspires to find ways to spend time alone with Cambridge. Just when Jessica is about to have her suspicions confirmed that her fiancé has been canoodling with her sister, Molly saves the day with a heartwarming alibi—the two of them have just been secretly planning a surprise that will make this the most epic wedding ever. Watching the couple make up, Molly chokes back a single, unselfish tear.

The alibi works until an hour before the church ceremony when Jessica gets lipstick on her veil and walks in on her sister and her fiancé dry-humping in the minister's private bathroom. The wedding off, chaos ensues: Jimmie, heartbroken, abandons Cambridge at the church and returns to their college alone; Jessica throws all of Doyle's possessions into the street outside their walkup; Cambridge tells Doyle that she had no idea that Jimmie was in love with her, and dashes back to college to make it up to him. After a torrent of Monique's finger-wagging I-told-you-so's, Doyle ends up in an all-night diner with his last friend in the world, his childhood pal Molly. Over burgers and shakes at three in the morning, he realizes that she's the love of his life and slips the wedding ring on her finger. The music comes up and we realize that true love always wins in the end.

What's intriguing about this plot is, actually, the fact that it's the apotheosis of predictability, packed with tropes so broadly drawn, they seem to be fighting each other to the death. Indeed, Hugh Grant's character is basically a boxing ring where the two great misogynist female caricatures of our generation, typified by Aniston and Deschanel, are meant to battle it out with each other, and perhaps it's a fortunate commentary on the future of cinema that neither of them win.

A sequel (titled either *A Bird in the Hand 2 In the Bush* or *A Bird in the Hand Two: In the Bush*) has been green-lit, this time, apparently, with Jennifer Aniston's character choosing between two suitors; one who's bad for her whom she lusts for, and one who's good for her whom she ignores. With the assumption that this sequel will meet expectations at the box office, and merely pass two hours of unmarked time on future international flights for years to come, they may use the studio's production budget to write everybody royalty checks in advance, and skip making the actual film.

Perhaps they're right to not do and say they did. Walking out of *A Bird in the Hand*, I was convinced that I never needed to see another movie again. So absolutely is this film about recycling— even codifying—a bland familiarity, it literally breaks one's unconscious desire to experience cinema, the way that the pureed meatloaf of a senior home dinner might make an octogenarian lose her memory of how to use a fork. In having neither Deschanel nor Aniston end up with Grant, it's a bit like telling the audience that you are not the winner here, that the film industry has been playing us for fools, and we like it. I was mildly disappointed, the way I used to be disappointed by airplane food or office Christmas parties—a disappointment mitigated by the understood quality of the holistic experience.

Then, less than a week later, I passed the poster at my bus stop and realized that I couldn't remember a single detail from the film. Within a day, were it not for the ticket stub I'd kept in my wallet, anyone could convince me that I never saw this movie at all. I actually had to see it again to write this review, and to my amazement, the theatre was packed, just like it was on opening weekend, and, I could swear, with many of the same people, and once again, all us walked in with mild anticipation and left with mild disappointment. I thought I was either batshit crazy or they were.

As it turns out, neither is true. My complete amnesia in regards to seeing this film turns out to be a widely experienced phenomenon across America. The film has been near the top of the box office for six weeks, and reason is that people are seeing the movie two, three, or even four times, forgetting they've seen it already.

So if you're still compelled to see *A Bird in the Hand*, fine. But for all of us who want to see an original movie again in our lifetimes, please keep your ticket stub in a place you see every day, or in your wallet, or on your dashboard, or stapled to the sleeve of your coat—whatever it takes. I, and the greater moviegoing public, thank you in advance, because we won't remember why.

SARAH TOMLINSON

FAMILY TIES

Directed by Alexander Payne. Written by Alexander Payne and Bob Nelson. Starring: Bryan Cranston, Naomi Watts, Ryan Gosling, Maggie Gyllenhaal, Dakota Fanning, and Benicio Del Toro.

"FAMILY IS NOT AN important thing, it's everything," once said that great cultural heavyweight, Michael J. Fox. He ought to know, having nursed his career at the bosom of two of the eighties' most iconic families: the McFlys of the popular *Back to the Future* franchise, and the Keaton clan of the beloved sitcom *Family Ties*. Perhaps no director would agree with this sentiment more these days than Alexander Payne. He has expanded his range of late by digging into the humor and pathos that is the chocolate and peanut butter of the dysfunctional family in several films about eccentric tribes and their relationships to their homelands, from Hawaii in *The Descendants* to his own home state of Nebraska in, well, *Nebraska*.

With pop-culture nostalgia at an all-time high (and studio creativity at an all time meh), it can seem like the truly landmark source material has already been plumbed for the big screen, from toys (*The Lego Movie*) and television shows (*The Dukes of Hazzard*, *The A-Team*) to commercials (while some felt the film adaptation of the iconic "Where's the Beef" TV ad was a bit thin, it must be acknowledged for its abundant laughs, thanks to a punchline that *never* gets old, and some surprisingly dark character work on the backstory of the "Where's the Beef" lady). So it's no surprise that not only the late, great action shows have made the leap to the big screen. The Wayans recently found abundant comic inspiration in *Family Matters*, while Wes Anderson discovered his own creative and aesthetic wellspring in *ALF*.

At a moment when our country's inflated higher educational system, limping economy, and high school population of aspiring porn stars mean it's no longer guaranteed that the current up-and-coming generation will do better than their parents, or even move out of their basements, this is the perfect moment to resurrect a TV family who found humor and drama in just such a generational divide. As originally conceived when the show first aired in 1982, at the family's head were former hippies Steven Keaton (Michael Gross) and Elyse Keaton (Meredith Baxter) whose children eschewed their liberal values in favor of Reaganomics, in the case of their young titan of industry Alex P. (Michael J. Fox), and in favor of image, in the case of their fashion-obsessed daughter Mallory (Justine Bateman), with younger daughter Jennifer (Tina Yothers) and son Andrew (Brian Bonsall) just wanting everyone to get along, which of course, in order to create sitcom gold, they did not, even if they *always* loved each other.

In his big screen adaptation, Payne was wise to focus less on the political specifics of the time, which would have risked turning the film into a historic set piece, and instead focus on the almost limitless potential for comic strife and ultimate familial redemption in the philosophical divide between liberals and conservatives. (What could be more of a hoot than your average session of Congress these days, right?) Tensions arise in the house when the local public television station run by Dad Steven (played by Bryan Cranston with remarkably understated charm in the style of the part's originator, nary a meth lab in sight) is threatened with the loss of NEA funding if it goes forward with plans to run a documentary about controversial artist Andres Serrano. As some will remember, Serrano's real-life work "Piss Christ" was at the center of a late-eighties cultural maelstrom over artistic and religious freedom, censorship, and what constitutes art. Of course, Alex (Ryan Gosling) does not believe the government should fund such "mumbo jumbo," not realizing his outspoken protest will ultimately cost his father his job. Fear not: conflict, and hilarity, ensue.

As with the original television show, much of the adaptation's success rests on the shoulders of its young star, who is given the best jokes and the most room to evolve as a character, showing as he does that there's more to a man than the way he fills out his sweater-vest. Unnamed sources have said that Gosling had to petition hard for the part, as Payne originally dismissed him as too "cool" to play Alex and was only wooed when Gosling sent the director a hand-shot audition of him decked out in a period Polo shirt, giving a believably chilling rendition of Reagan's infamous "Evil Empire" speech in support of armament against Godless Communism. For his part, Gosling has been quoted as saying of the role of Alex, "I've played alcoholics, sociopaths, and womanizers, but I wanted to challenge myself with a part that was the least like me *and* the most bleak: a Reagan-era conservative." Gosling has also said in multiple interviews that as a fellow Canadian, Michael J. Fox has long been a hero and a major inspiration behind his career, as well as the occasional haircut.

With no disrespect to the original source material, which managed to sneak in some smart social commentary amid running gags about who in the household was hogging the telephone and Alex's love of money, the script here, cowritten by Payne and his *Nebraska* collaborator, Bob Nelson, goes deeper and darker. Their adaptation gets inside the angst of father-son discord as it dates back to "Death of a Salesman" and even further to Psalm 153: "Fear not, father, for I can milk that camel on my own, and now I am a man." The story is not so much about the specifics of plot and its resolution but more about how each individual character grows during that necessary moment at which parents must be pushed off their pedestals in order for children to grow into their own people, and the specific ways in which respect and love are engendered within a family (i.e., guilt).

Other cinematic bonbons worth mentioning include Naomi Watts' wig, which gives her just the lustrous mop once sported by Baxter. Benicio Del Toro's delightfully derelict turn as Mallory's much-dissed, lug-headed boyfriend, Nick, who suggests he's got more brains than he'd dare to let on amid this group of wannabe eggheads. And Gyllenhaal as Mallory, who, much like Bateman's original portrayal shows that sometimes ignorance is its own form of grace. But in the end, the film is an ensemble piece, and its best moments, as in real life, are when the whole family is together, scrapping and soothing, threatening to almost veer into the sentimental, but always saved at the last minute by Payne's deft observation of the truest truth there is: family is about more than just blood, it's about guts. If Payne doesn't win an Academy Award for this film, it'll be the greatest Oscar travesty since Dame Judi Dench's "Where's the Beef" lady lost to Fran Drescher in *The Nanny Takes Reno.*

MICHAEL MARTONE

KODAK: THE FILM

Directed by Martin Scorsese. Narrated by Bill Cosby.

A WEEK BEFORE THE iconic film and camera company received the dire warning from Wall Street, threatening the delisting of its shares from the New York Stock Exchange, *Kodak: The Film* opened a limited run to a disappointing box office in select theaters in Los Angeles and Rochester, New York. The film, *Kodak: The Film* was filmed on what is thought to be the last remaining film stock of Kodak's VISION3 200T Color Negative Film 5213/7213, a formulation the company had hoped would compete with the evolving and less expensive tape and digital recording formats. Found stored in what was once the RKO Radio Pictures Studio building in Culver City, later purchased by Desilu Productions and now an independent postproduction facility, the Kodak film of *Kodak: The Film* is iridescent and shockingly vivid in the visual and sonic information it conveys.

Kodak: The Film stars no one really but the material means of production of photographic reproduction—cameras, chemicals, emulsifiers, negatives, filters, film—exposed and not. Narrated by the comedian and educator Bill Cosby, who was at one time the company's commercial spokesman, *Kodak: The Film* might be thought of as a documentary docudrama hybrid. It is a 3-D, super-color-saturated version of *March of the Penguins* spliced with the sixteen-millimeter coarsely grained black-and-white capitalist-socialist realistic propagandistic shorts made during the Cold War by the AFL-CIO called *Industry on Parade*.

Though these primogenitors suggest movement, what is most striking about *Kodak: The Film* is that it is a movie that does not move shot, as it is a series of stills. The static motion technique of *Kodak: The Film* harkens back to the haunting 1962 film, *La Jetee*, by Chris Marker who acted, at ninety-two, as a consultant to

Kodak: The Film's director Martin Scorsese. The technique teaches the viewer, as the slide show slides by, the filmstrip nature of the film as the film is stripped of its essential illusion of movement. We are asked to appreciate the apparent invisible vibrant and constant nature of light itself, both wave and particle.

Kodak: The Film is itself haunting as it haunts itself, opening as it does with a photomontage of superimposed "found" images salvaged from dumpsters near photo processing labs where snapshots were discarded by their owners. Thousands of pictures of random people posing (one after the other), waving, dissolving into pictures of people in costume—for Halloween, the prom, weddings, first communions—fading into one hundred years of birthdays—the cakes on the tables, the air made madly solid by the spent candle smoke caught drifting, illuminated by Instamatic flash cubes that are themselves pictured flashing and turning and revealing, in the red afterglow of the flash, picture after picture of people taking pictures of people taking pictures, the floating pinpoints of light coming to light on the contracted irises of red-eyed starry-eyed startled pets that bleed into the overexposed nebula of nebulous social gatherings, graduations, gardens, grandstands, gratuitous sexual organs.

Kodak: The Film is a paean to point-of-view, to point-and-shoot, as the camera pans and pulls, tracks and racks. One is submerged in this new sublime subliminal atmosphere of aperture and f-stop. The light here is a liquid ceaselessly flowing, arranging itself in pixelated patterns that sort themselves into image after image of images of images of actual water of light falling over the High Falls of the Genesee River in headwaters of the river of film, Rochester, NY.

Finally, there is finally, no finality to *Kodak: The Film*. It is all collage and cutting. One jumps over the chasm of invisible darkness between the frames, the stutter steps over the stepping-stones, the endless loops, the speeds of stillness going nowhere fast. *Kodak: The Film* is the filmiest film school film filmed. Another section of the film highlights film leaders. It becomes a kind of film-within-a-film film. A number of film leaders, their numbers counting down, lead to a film of numbers counting down. There is a poignant collection of hand-scratched changeover cue marks that promise reels of film that never arrive. The somber *Kodak: The Film* is both record and method of the annihilation of space and time before our eyes. It ends not as a consequence of consequence, nor through the machinations of plot or narrative of cause and effect or character drive or growth or change. *Kodak: The Film* ends in entropy; its final montage sequence pitted against our perceived notion of sequential time.

The movie's whole and wholly on-message message has been this stunning relentless resistance. No beginning. No middle. No end. The final sequence consumes itself, a rapid-fire firing of the artifact of plastic time catching fire. Pictured are frames after frames of frames spontaneously combusting, melting, literally dissolving, evaporating, jammed and jellied, reduced and rendered, boiled and fried, warped and scorched, effaced, vaporized before your eyes. The sprocket holes gape open like the scream in *The Scream*. This goes on for hours. I mean for hours literally, in homage to Andy Warhol's 1964 film *Empire*, the camera does not look away from this serial sizzling stasis. You are steeped in the banality of boredom, of the repeating images of images of time-lapsed explosion, implosion, of the deep breathing and frustrated sighing of Bill Cosby on the frayed and fraying soundtrack. But you do not want to look away because (spoiler alert!) the next frozen image of decay might actually be the actual animation of *Kodak: The Film*'s self-destruction as all of the prints (and now there are so few left to see) are treated to ignite of their own volition, sooner or later, and disappear completely into volatile vapors and very little ash.

ADAM CUSHMAN

OUTLAW COUNTRY

Directed by Bennett Miller. Starring: Ryan Gosling, John Hawkes, Joel Edgerton, Tom Berenger, James McAvoy, Walton Goggins, Shelley Duvall, Christopher Walken, and Jeffrey Dean Morgan as Johnny Cash.

THE QUESTION IS NOT, what is Outlaw Country? For those unfamiliar with the term, it's a genre of country music created by country legends Willie Nelson, Johnny Cash, Merle Haggard, Kris Kristofferson, Jerry Jeff Walker, and Waylon Jennings in the late 1960's as a reaction to the softening of Nashville honky-tonk and an exploration into the purity of free living men. The film *Outlaw Country* is also that sort of exploration, and, like the musical style from which its name derives, it exists outside of the system, while remaining an intrinsic part of it. Much like the irony of a movie like *Fight Club* being made by Fox, when you watch *Outlaw Country,* you'll wonder how the hell Paramount ever agreed to make it, but you'll give thanks to God that they did.

This isn't just the study of a largely unknown offshoot of country music. It's the celebration of a man: the late great Waylon Jennings.

The film opens on a dark airstrip in 1959, outside a single-engine plane, as young Waylon gives his seat away to The Big Bopper (Jason Segel, who put on forty pounds for this one scene). Ritchie Valens (Michael Peña) boards the plane and Buddy Holly (Jay Baruchel) tells Waylon, "I hope your ol' bus freezes up," to which Waylon replies, "Well, Buddy, I hope your ol' plane crashes." Then Holly offers the slightest of smirks to Waylon, who was Holly's bass player on the "Winter Dance Party" tour, and Waylon watches the plane move down the jet way.

Then we see Waylon's face for the first time as a single tear falls down his cheek. This version of Waylon is portrayed by actor Ryan Gosling. It's worth a mention because it's also the last time we'll see Gosling.

Director Bennett Miller explains: "A lot of people are comparing this to Todd's (Haynes) movie *I'm Not There.* I just don't think that's a fair comparison."

Miller is referring to Haynes casting six radically different actors in his interpretation of the life and work of Bob Dylan. Miller took it a step further in his choice of recasting Waylon in every scene. That's right. In the Waylon Jennings biopic, the legendary country music star is portrayed by no fewer than forty-seven actors, most notably Gosling, Marlon Wayans, Michael Fassbender, Judy Davis, John Hawkes, Guy Pearce, Ben Mendelsohn, and Christopher Walken.

Walken said in a recent article in *EW*, "Guys, when I was a boy, all I wanted was to be Waylon Jennings. I was a song and dance man. Country boy deep down. Inside."

Which, okay, makes no sense since a) Jennings was only six years older than Walken and wasn't performing until Walken was a grown man, and b) Mr. Walken is from Queens.

Miller, who also wrote the screenplay for *Outlaw Country*, explains, "What Chris is saying is this is a movie that breaks the biographical mold. A lot of what you see may confuse you. Sometimes it confuses me. If you're looking for a straight-up narrative you can sum up in a Netflix review, go watch *Walk the Line*. Or fuckin' *Blackthorn*, *Bloodheart*, *Crazy Mouth*, I get them all mixed up myself. This ain't that movie. This is a tribute to a man who was riding a big blue ball. He never did dream that he would fall."

"He's [Miller] been doing that since we started shooting," says producer Michael De Luca. First it was the hick accent. Then he's directing the actors using song lyrics, mostly from *Luckenbach, Texas*. We were shooting the scene where Waylon storms out of the USA for Africa recording session. Waylon was played by John Hawkes in the scene. John asks Bennett what was Waylon's motivation for you know, hightailing it. Bennett gets right up in John's face and sings, '*The successful life we're livin's got us feuding like the Hatfields and McCoys.*' And you know what? John knew exactly what he meant. It's a fucking intense scene."

Wracked with guilt for thinking his words gave way to "The Day the Music Died," Waylon turns to amphetamines to ease the burden.

He meets Willie Nelson (James McAvoy) in a recording session, and the two become fast friends, recording several albums together in the film's record-breaking forty-five minute montage, culminating in the 1980's, when Willie and Waylon (now played by Ving Rhames) join forces with Kris Kristofferson (Joel Edgerton) and Johnny Cash (Jeffrey Dean Morgan) as the super band The Highwaymen.

But these moments from Waylon's life aren't part of a narrative flow of any kind, as Miller pointed out. The whole film, much like Waylon lived, plays like one long moment, interspersed with nuggets of truth, plenty of myth, and journeys to space.

The astronaut scene is going to be Bennett Miller's *Tree of Life* dinosaur.

Without giving too much away, it features Val Kilmer as a bearded Waylon, floating through the big empty with a meditative glare behind his space mask as "Old Five and Dimers (Like Me)" twists our hearts like gasoline soaked rags, reminding us we've lost our way. The scene itself is breathtaking and, pardon me for going all wine and cheese, no one's going to understand it.

"No one understands why it's there. No one. Waylon Jennings did not travel to outer space. That is a fact," says Outlaw member Jerry Jeff Walker, who's played by Walton Goggins.

Parts of the film feel like someone just turned a camera on in the middle of Waylon's life and pointed it at him.

One scene begins with Waylon (William Zabka) flushing cocaine down the toilet as Federal agents and NYPD cops storm the recording studio.

Cut to Waylon (Peter Stormare) backstage watching Johnny sing "Orange Blossom Special" and take two vicious pulls off his bullet.

And each scene gives birth to the next.

Now Waylon's played by his real-life son, country singer Shooter Jennings, as he strolls lakeside with Shel Silverstein (Ciarán Hinds) discussing firm feeling women, diabetes, and getting old.

Miller is saying in essence that life doesn't contain a narrative you can squeeze into two hours, not in a way that would make any real sense. Our lives are a catalogue of moments and that's what we think makes us who we are.

Taking a swig from his whiskey glass, Miller strokes his long beard and says, "We all cling to this idea of ourselves. I'm this, I'm that, that's not like me, I don't feel like myself today. It's all a bunch of bullshit. We ain't anyone. Yet we are the world. We are the people. We are... Oh wait, he didn't...he didn't sing that song, never mind, never mind, I got confused."

"They should have called this movie *The Day the Music Lived*," Kristofferson said on a call from his home in Santa Fe. "For a whole lot of reasons. Hasn't been a film that understands the spirit of country since Bob Altman shot *Nashville* in 1974."

Actor Shelley Duvall, who plays Jennings' fourth wife Jessi Colter in *Outlaw Country* and was also the star of *Nashville,* said her favorite part of the film is *The Dukes of Hazzard* sequence. Waylon did the theme song for the 1980's hit TV show, as well as the narration as the balladeer. In the film, Miller recreates the making of a scene where Waylon (William Forsythe) plays "Never Could Toe the Mark" for the whole cast, including Anthony Michael Hall and Bronson Pinchot as Bo and Luke Duke, Tom Wilkinson as Uncle Jesse, Evangeline Lilly as Daisy, Brad Dourif as Roscoe, and Richard Dreyfuss as Boss Hogg. "I loved it," Duvall said, "It's a performance in a TV show in a movie about the man giving the performance. It's a circle. Just like life is. And it all circles back to Waylon."

"It's about identity," said Tom Berenger, who plays the final version of Waylon walking off stage in his last performance, slow-mowing it in his leather vest and black cowboy hat, carrying his 1953 Telecaster down the hall into the blinding white lights. "And not Waylon's identity, it's about Bennett's. This movie is as much about him as it is the man who left his boot print on country music forever. Look at him. Look what happened to him."

"Sure," Miller said, "ain't no doubt this guy got inside me, rearranged my soul, him and his music did that shit to me. But there are many men in me. You understand what I'm saying? It's like this: remember the son a bitch who shot Lennon? Why'd he say he did it? Because he loved him so much he was becoming him. He had to do it. To save his own life. This movie, is the opposite of the assassination of John Lennon. We took all that love Waylon gave us and we made something."

Walken elucidates, "Everything he says, it's crazy. Guy told me the other day why he chose me to play Waylon, says it's because we both got six letters in our names. Says it's like Jesus and Elvis. Guess that makes me the son of God."

When we finally asked Miller if he thought Waylon Jennings would relate to this (at best) loose interpretation of his days, he smiled, put on a black cowboy hat, and slow walked out of the interview.

His publicist says he's holed up in his trailer in Luckenbach, Texas, waiting for Willie and the boys.

ANA OTTMAN

PLANET OF THE WOMEN

Directed by Jill Soloway. Written by Margaret Atwood, Shonda Rhimes, and Jill Soloway. Starring: Meryl Streep, Kerry Washington, Ellen Page, Jamie Chung, Laverne Cox, Emma Watson, Malala Yousafzai, Roxane Gay, Malia Obama, Margaret Cho, Tavi Gevinson, Lidia Yuknavitch, RuPaul, Zoe Saldana, Mindy Kaling, Gaby Hoffman, Kristen Wiig, and Oprah.

"THE MEN HAD THEIR chance," says Virginia Carr (Meryl Streep). "And just look at what they did. It's time for us to rise."

Many an EMILY's List member has fantasized about what it would be like to have a society led exclusively by women, but no one was brave enough to tackle it on the big screen—until now. Written and directed by Jill Soloway (*Transparent, Afternoon Delight*), this utopian movie answers the question that no man in a position of power has asked, like ever: WWWD? (What would women do?)

When the corrupt, colonialist male-led United States government brings the country to its knees in 2025 after spending billions of dollars on oil-related wars and giving tax breaks to the wealthy, rolling back reproductive rights, granting personhood to corporations, and decimating social services and education systems, an underground sect of militant feminists stages a coup.

With a non-hierarchical power structure and consensus decision making, the group, who call themselves "Pussy Power" internally and just "The Women" externally, begin recruiting on November 9, 2016. They start in the obvious hotbeds of feminist bookstores and women's studies departments, and quickly branch out to disseminating coded messages through carpool lines at schools, on Pinterest, and in book clubs.

The movie opens with a group of women who are preparing to go into battle by watching Beyoncé's *Lemonade*. During the coup, instead of action-heavy fight sequences, we see women taking long walks while having pointed conversations with male leaders, explaining that *they're* going to have to take over now. The actresses go about their days giving direct, explicit instructions to men and having intimate conversations with their closest confidantes. The coup is a success and comes off with minimal deaths and almost no violence—mostly Gaby Hoffman kicking Steve Bannon repeatedly in the balls.

As punishment, the deposed male leaders and white women who voted for Trump are imprisoned in a room with speakers playing Audre Lorde, bell hooks, and Judith Butler, and made to study a diagram of the female reproductive system. The prisoners are not allowed to leave until they can correctly recite the tenants of intersectional feminist theory, describe how a woman's reproductive system works, be trained in anti-racism, and explain the spectrum of sexuality and gender. (Some men are held captive for years.)

To run the country after the coup, the position of president rotates among The Women members. The cabinet is easily established by matching members' innate callings with the needs of the country. Malala Yousafzai leads education, Emma Watson oversees humanitarian efforts, Oprah guides economic empowerment, Kerry Washington leads strategy and damage control, Ellen Page runs intelligence services with Laverne Cox directing bullshit detection, Malia Obama and Tavi Gevinson are the youth organizers, RuPaul and Margaret Cho lead positive self-image efforts, and Roxane Gay and Lydia Yuknavitch promote literacy and literature. The first official action taken by the new government is a sincere public apology to indigenous peoples whose land we've settled on and the immediate upholding of all treaties made with the various indigenous nations, including the return of sacred sites.

Problems arise when conditions for Americans improve so drastically, including a dramatic rise in both the GDP and the newly created Gross National Happiness (GNH), that male leaders from other countries start to worry that similar uprisings might take place in their own nations. Soloway has women play the likeness of several male leaders, including Kristen Wiig as Vladmir Putin, who, having thought he silenced Pussy Riot and their ilk, was heard to saying, "These bitches again?"

This entire concept could have been pulled directly from Bill O'Reilly's nightmares. It's been widely reviewed elsewhere, with

Los Angeles Times film critic Kenneth Turan calling it "a puzzling feminist fantasyland" and *Slate*'s Dana Stevens commenting: "It's got everything—complex characters across a representative spectrum and a sense of justice being served. One commenter on the YouTube trailer with the username "clockworkorange" said: "wtf. this isn't real, is it? everyone knows girls can't be in charge because they go psycho during their periods."

Sources also reveal that Tom Junod was practically salivating to write his own review in *Esquire,* following up his "In Praise of 42-Year-Old Women" piece where he wrote: "In truth, it is feminism that has made forty-two-year-old women so desirable." On *Planet of the Women,* he continues his theme, anointing feminists with his latest approval because "it is not popular." He writes "The carnal appeal of this movie is that the women don't need us, and that makes us want them even more."

When asked about her inspiration for the project, Soloway said: "Witnessing an orange menace get elected president in 2016, instead of the most qualified candidate we've had in decades whose gender seemed to infuriate people, made me feel hopeless about the direction this country was headed. I started fantasizing about how different this country would be if women were in charge, and the story came to me easily from there."

"When I heard Jill was writing this script, I knew I wanted in," said Streep. "What woke woman wouldn't want the chance to shape a country that eliminates toxic power systems instead of constantly feeling like a pawn in men's demented ego games?"

Though male leaders around the world attempt to block Pussy Power's efforts to contact women in other countries, by the end of the movie we see the seeds of uprising begin to grow, mostly through Twitter.

Let's just say, I wouldn't be surprised if a whole franchise begins here, and expect *These Bitches Again: Planet of the Women* to be in preproduction shortly.

JIMMY CHEN

ROSEMARY'S BABY

Directed by Woody Allen. Starring: Woody Allen, Mia Farrow, Jerry Stiller, Estelle Harris, Haley Joel Osment, Steve Carell, and Paul Rudd.

WHEN WOODY ALLEN ANNOUNCED he would be remaking *Rosemary's Baby* (1968) as a comedy, various heated claims that he was doing so purely out of spite for Mia Farrow were tweeted fifty-three times by his estranged son, Ronan Farrow, in less than two hours; meanwhile, Hollywood insiders wondered if the elderly director—whose earlier work was constantly punctuated by meta-aware fourth wall breaks—had taken irony too far, as he and Mia Farrow were partners for twelve years, a relationship which ended disastrously when the latter discovered photos of her then twenty-year-old adopted daughter Soon-Yi in the former's possession.

"My f-final c-c-comedy," said the seventy-eight-year-old director, reappropriating his stage stutter during his acceptance speech for the AFI Lifetime Achievement Award, which was met with a standing ovation. "Do you all like me that much, or is it just hemorrhoids?" The audience roared with laughter.

After an austere late period marked by brilliant yet nefarious tales of murder and deceit (*Match Point*), codependence and adultery (*Vicky Cristina Barcelona*), and a huge nervous breakdown (*Blue Jasmine*), it was nice to hear Allen returning to the comedic form of his earlier farces like *Love & Death*, *Sleeper*, and *Zelig*. As a gesture of solidarity to the original writer, he even asked Roman Polanski—who is not known for comedy, but who notably mimicked Allen's humor—to reimagine a zanier and more upbeat screenplay.

Jerry Stiller and Estelle Harris reprise their Seinfeldian roles as the overbearing Costanzas, only this time as the neighboring Castevet devil worshipers. When Jerry Stiller (as Roman Castevet) barges in the apartment à la the explosive mannerisms of *Seinfeld*'s Kramer, Rosemary seems like a subdued pre-feminist version of the more confrontational Elaine Benes. As unbelievable the present-day Woody Allen and Mia Farrow are as the Woodhouses—and through the sheer resentment you can see in their eyes, perhaps in the Method acting of life's disaster—there is still a faint touch of empathy, or at least resignation, in their fake address to each other. The unhappy marriage is made more surreal and disturbing by Polanski's attempt at Allenean humor:

GUY WOODHOUSE:

Where's my Viagra?

ROSEMARY WOODHOUSE:

I put it in the cactus, dear.

GUY WOODHOUSE:

Somebody call a doctor, it's been over four hours!

In "Letter from 'Manhattan'" (*The New York Review of Books*, August 16, 1979) Joan Didion facetiously notes how the rather self-absorbed characters in his "serious" work (*Annie Hall, Interiors,* and *Manhattan*) all "seem to take long walks and go to smart restaurants only to ask one another hard questions," which is both admittedly accurate yet sadly hypocritical if one considers Didion's frequent preoccupation with her own intellectual bourgeois lifestyle, of which she is most critical in Allen, going so far to call his characters "faux adults." True, in this remake of *Rosemary's Baby* we do indeed meet a bickering upper-class couple, of Jew and WASP binary, arguing about where to hang the Damien Hirst dot painting; if the lobster ravioli needs more sage; if the rare orchids have been watered, among many other economically ostentatious qualms. Allen here, as a common crutch, "goes off" on Hegel, Freud, and Marx—losing himself not as Guy Woodhouse but, literally, as *himself*, to a stunned Rosemary holding a pregnancy test.

Woody Allen and Roman Polanski sadly have one more thing in common, besides muse Mia Farrow. Their collaboration here, however perverse, passive-aggressive, or misogynistic, has hit mass market regardless. *People* magazine, for idiot populace, called it "the one movie to watch this summer." BuzzFeed captured twenty-seven of the film's most climactic GIFs, which, according to them, will make your head explode.

Perhaps most frightening, as opposed to the original version in which the baby's face was never portrayed, is Haley Joel Osment as Satan's spawn. Osment—best known for his "I see dead people" line in *The Sixth Sense*—is twenty-six years old now, and despite his "baby face," not to mention some rather expensive and tedious CGI, a very horrendous-looking baby. The penultimate shot, before Rosemary faints and punctures her colostomy bag with a broken hip, is a lone zoom in on Osment in heavy goth makeup trying to facialize the embodiment of evil. Some laughed, others gasped, a few gagged.

Cameos by Steve Carell and Paul Rudd as the gay neighbors raised lips a little, but ultimately Polanski should not be writing dick jokes. The Victorian Gothic interiors were indeed stunning, but Allen's camera seems more loyal to the product placements (Depend, Preparation H, Sensodyne, Welch's Prune juice, etc). The Woodhouses' geriatric gait never quite matches up to the snappy cadence of the jazz soundtrack, which continuously blows its cacophonous horns into laugh tracks inserted by a director clearly at the end of his game. Maybe this is a horror film after all.

SARA FINNERTY

TWO THOUSAND AND FOURTEEN

Directed by Social Media. Length: 1440 minutes.
Starring: the general public.

TWO THOUSAND AND FOURTEEN is a genre-bending, logic-defying, not-to-be-missed, nearly-impossible-to-watch moviegoing experience released by a third-party team of anonymous programmers at Facebook, Google, and Twitter. Officially directed by a location-based randomized search engine, *Two Thousand and Fourteen* can only be seen in theaters, and will never be released on video.

Much has been written about *Two Thousand and Fourteen* (*TTAF*), and even months before its release, it was hotly debated in the highest-minded critic circles. Let's get the specifics out of the way, on the highly improbable off-chance that you have not been made aware of this moviegoing juggernaut. *TTAF* is a twenty-four-hour-long film with a list of demands attached to the ticket. Audience members must arrive on time, sit through the entirety of the film, and only use the allotted prearranged bathroom breaks. They may not sleep and must be fully engaged for the entirety of the twenty-four hours. The film consists of the six top-grossing films of 2014 interspersed with the bottom-grossing yet highly acclaimed movies of 2014. The film will be accompanied by written commentary on the individual movies compiled from Google searches, email and messaging content, Facebook commentary and private messages, and Twitter scrapes, all culled from a fifty-mile radius of the theater. In essence, *TTAF* will be a totally different experience based on where in the country the film is being watched. It is the most important experience of our time.[1]

---

1   Full disclosure: author did not see the film.

Tickets to this life-altering event[2] are in the vicinity of $300 per person and include unlimited popcorn and soda.

Whenever possible, the same sources will be used as commentary for different movies that compose the film. For example, if a Twitter user in Chicago tweets, "*Twilight* is a piece of shit," and, later, that same user tweets, "*Down in the Dirt in Texas* changed my life," both commentaries will be used during the film.[3]

There has been some controversy about the length and price of *TTAF*. In some cities there are reports of the film playing to empty theaters (which is in itself a fascinating thought experiment). But in cities where tickets are often sold out, audience participation adds a whole other dimension to the film. For example, Wikipedia reports that in a Brooklyn screening of *TTAF*, during one of the top-grossing movies, a local woman's Facebook post appeared on the screen: "Do we really need to see Jennifer Lawrence in another modern-day fairy tale steeped in dark mythology, turning the trope of woman-as-victim into one of woman-as-hero? I mean must we sit through this?" When the post appeared on the screen, the East Williamsburg crowd erupted into cheers.

These are the meta-moments *TTAF* bring to us, and these moments change our lives. We realize that we are sitting in a movie theater with like-minded moviegoers, all able and willing to pay for a $300 ticket, brought together by social media and the Internet. During a San Francisco screening[4], upon the opening credits of *Gothic Love Nest*, a snippet of an email appeared on screen: "Why do they make these movies? Do we really need another movie

---

2   For the purpose of clarity, hereafter the twenty-four-hour event will be referred to as a "film." The twelve components of the film will be referred to as "movies."

3   Surely everyone on earth will agree with these two statements.

4   As reported by a blog on the internet.

about teenagers falling in love? Come on! Real women don't fall in love!" This commentary was also met with approval in the theater.

Some versions of *TTAF* are presented for hours without commentary, as many people in a particular town or area will never have heard of a number of the movies. Even if some of these townspeople, most likely in remote areas of the country, happen to watch the film, how will they know what to think about certain movies, if said movies are presented without commentary? This leads one to ponder the sad life of those who do not live in major cities.

There have also been reports of charities offering to foot the $300 bill in areas where the film plays to empty houses. "I have a life to live, no thank you," one woman said. "I don't want to be forced to sit through movies I'm not interested in," said an ornery old man. "I'll just watch what I want, when I want. I'm sure others are capable of doing the same."[5]

The lesson this reviewer comes away with is that one cannot force culture on a people, and one cannot force a consciousness shift, and that escapism of any kind is the ultimate insult to life as we know it.

---

5   This may appear to be a reasonable statement, but where would we be as a society if we didn't give our opinions and critique to media for which we were never the intended audience?

MIKE SACKS

LOST CLASSICS! THE RAREST OF THE RARE!

WOW, WHAT AN AMAZING year! I want to thank each and every one of you readers for checking my blog Unknown-Celluloid-Classics. net. With your help, and a tiny mention in the *Maryland Film Fanatic* zine, the site has now reached more than two thousand weekly readers! Exciting stuff.

I also wanted to thank you by giving you a "best of." What follows are my favorite reviews of "lost" and "cult" movies that I was privileged enough to have told all of you about. Don't forget! You heard about these from me first!

In no particular order:

Andy Warhol's *Bowel Movement*

This is a good one and ultra, ultra rare. In 1967, Andy Warhol filmed himself sitting on the toilet for an entire year. He ate, slept and, yes, went toilet. The film is shot in real time and will take you an entire year to watch, but there's an abbreviated version that runs about four months. I don't recommend that version, as you'd be missing out on some really key plot points. The movie was shot on eight-millimeter, in black and white, with a soundtrack by the amazing 1960s band Young Man With a Flower, featuring a very, very young Phil Collins. Good luck finding the soundtrack, which is worth about fifty dollars! If you're not doing anything for a year and need a fun way to pass the time, you could definitely do a hell of a lot worse.

Styx: Live at the Capitol Center, September 5, 1989

This bootleg was shot on a VHS camera by a man from Potomac, Maryland. The man's name is lost to history, but we can thank him for preserving the last Styx tour before Dennis DeYoung caught a rare Amazonian virus (fishing nude in Brazil) and left the group to start a boutique candle business.

Everyone knows that Styx is best remembered for their amazing and fully realized concept album *Kilroy Was Here*. But what everyone does not realize is that Styx released another rock opera, this one in 1989, that was also about robots. In this case, the robots take over an ice cream shop in Atlanta. They refuse to serve vanilla or chocolate ice cream for political reasons, and the locals go insane. Dennis DeYoung plays Stuey, an assistant manager who appeals to the community through song and gentle hand movements.

In the beginning of this 1989 concert, Dennis is wearing an orange and brown smock and he is holding an ice cream scooper. He then launches into the album's biggest hit, "Bathroom's Only for Lovers." At the end of the concert, Dennis is wearing a yellow suit and is singing "Flavor of the Day: Happiness." It's a fantastic concert and ultra, ultra, ULTRA rare. Known to sell on eBay for as high as forty-five dollars.

Dennis DeYoung died a few years ago. He packed a ton of love into those eighty-three years.

The Shining: The Completely Unedited Cut

Stanley Kubrick was never completely satisfied with the final cut of 1980's *The Shining*, so he released the movie into a few German theaters in 1991 with this unedited version. No one showed up at those screenings, and no one has seen this version since (unfortunately, his wife locked it away in a vault), but it's rumored to have an entirely new ending: Jack Torrance, now back in the world of 1927, wants to make money, so he invents the cheese-in-the-crust pizza and becomes fabulously rich. He also invests in Apple and pets.com. One out of two ain't bad! That's all I know. If you have a copy, email me!

M. Night Shyamalan's Unnamed Third, Fifth and Seventh Projects

Shyamalan is a genius, I don't think there's much argument over that fact. What's not well known is that he wrote, directed and released three projects that went straight to video:

The Fateful Night of the Rainbow Catcher (2001)

The Moist Stump (2003)

Intergalactic Hugs (2011)

Here are the twists for each of these movies:
Fudge doesn't melt at that temperature. Also, that wasn't fudge.
Wood sprites are incapable of growing large afros.
It wasn't the retarded guy who lives in the woods. Actually, it was the retarded guy who lives in the woods.

I pray that all of these will one day be released. Shyamalan is a brilliant auteur, very humble, and he deserves a lot more respect and recognition.

Jerry Lewis's *The Day the Clown Went to Rwanda*

For the entire decade of the nineties, Jerry Lewis was hooked on methadone. Because of that, he has no memory making this movie that he wrote, directed, and starred in. The movie is called *The Day the Clown Went to Rwanda*, and that's basically the entire plot. Jerry—playing an unemployed clown named Wolfgart—travels to Rwanda to cheer up the poor orphans who will soon face their own grisly deaths. Wolfgart performs magic tricks, walks a tightrope (only a few feet off the ground), and sprays water out of his fake bowtie and into the mud. The kids really laugh. Three people have seen this movie, including a former reviewer for *The Washington Post*, Anthony Hoagland, who wrote: "Like watching a snuff film but without the laughs."

I think that's way, way too harsh, but having never seen this movie, I can't really prove otherwise. I do know that it was all shot in Jerry's backyard in Las Vegas and features no one of color.

Pluckett & Farley

Burt Reynolds is amazingly prolific. He has starred in over three hundred movies and about two hundred TV shows. He never stops. Burt was especially in his prime in the mid-seventies, but no one seems to have ever seen *Pluckett & Farley*, even though it's available on Blockbuster streaming. I do know that the movie was shown at an Alabama drive-in theater in '76 and never seen again. The rumor is that the guy who owned the drive-in traded the movie for enough money to keep the drive-in going for another month, after which it immediately went out of business for good.

I'm a sucker for any movie that features intelligent orangutans doing human things, like giving a thumbs-up, blowing a raspberry, or just mouthing off to racist cops.

This movie has none of that, but it does feature a really beautiful orangutan named Farley who was rescued somewhere in Africa and then purchased by Burt for $200 at a Kentucky Derby party.

Whenever Farley gets mad or scared, he attacks everything in sight and rips off limbs. If that doesn't sound funny, rest assured that it's hilarious on the screen.

In one scene, Burt (who plays Pluckett) tells Farley to fetch him a beer. Farley goes the fridge but comes back with a soda. Burt kicks Farley out of the house. Farley then goes on a rampage, attempting to kill anyone who tries to stop him, including a redneck sheriff and an uppity woman who hates alcohol. Both die, but it's okay, as both weren't very nice. (It's interesting: in the novelization to this film, the orangutan is played by a donkey. Not sure why they changed it.)

The movie ends with Farley being put down by a zookeeper in a helicopter as Burt stands before a gorgeous sunset and weeps. There was no sequel.

Side note: I saw this movie in the basement of a movie theater. I'm friends with the manager and we like to use his office for watching movies while the new (and lame) movies are playing upstairs. Anyway, after watching *Pluckett & Farley*, I was so jazzed, so excited by what I had just seen (that very few others ever had) that I ran up to the lobby and started yelling to the people coming out of Tyler Perry's *Good Deeds*. No one seemed particularly interested. This happens all the time.

Folks, that is the best of the best! If you're feeling generous, please donate to the site! Unearthing these gems ain't free.

Bootleg Mike
RARESHITBOOTS@yahoo.com

PAUL DURICA

HOME ALONE: REPOSSESSED

Directed by Phil Lord and Chris Miller. Starring: Macaulay Culkin, Catherine O'Hara, John Heard, Joe Pesci, Daniel Stern, and Alan Ruck.

REMEMBER A COUPLE OF months back when photos began to surface of an emaciated and bearded Macaulay Culkin, leading to speculation that the former child star was drug-addled, destitute, or some combination of the two? Mac stayed mum, but directors Phil Lord and Chris Miller (*21 Jump Street*) ended the speculation when they announced that Culkin was getting into character and that they would be making what is technically the sixth installment in the *Home Alone* franchise. But does America really need to go Home again? Can such a premise hold any charm for audiences too young to remember the first films or too old to not be disillusioned by the intervening years?

Home Alone: Repossessed opens with a quick succession of scenes in which the now adult Kevin McCallister (Culkin) loses his job at an unnamed tech firm, his beautiful and much younger fiancée, and lastly his soulless, sprawling box of a house somewhere in the Las Vegas suburbs. Reduced to some home office furniture, a flat-screen TV, and several boxes of Annie's organic mac & cheese, Kevin is rescued, as it were, from the Great Recession by the fortuitous timing of a phone call from his parents and a Tivo'd movie. It seems that the elder MacCallisters (Catherine O'Hara and John Heard, squandered in what amounts to little more than a cameo) are away on a second honeymoon cruise in Alaska. After watching *Angels with the Dirtiest Faces of Them All* late one night and seeing one of the gangster characters evade capture by hiding out in an abandoned house, Kevin gets a brilliant idea: he's going to return to Illinois, break into his temporarily empty childhood home, and survive there for as long as he can. In a neat twist, the former defender of the domestic has now become an invader.

Culkin is thirty-three and wears his years well. There's a brilliant moment early in the film when Kevin awakes in his practically empty house, trudges into the bathroom, and goes through what is essentially shot-for-shot the same sequence from the first *Home Alone*. Those of us old enough to remember that film will no doubt feel a lump in our collective throats when Kevin splashes the aftershave on his cheeks without the slightest reaction. He simply stares for a moment in the mirror and then runs his hands through his thinning hair before pinching a blackhead on his brow. Here is a portrait of a man who has lost faith in himself and the world.

Adding to Kevin's problems is the inevitable return of the Wet Bandits. A parallel plotline follows the parole of Harry (Joe Pesci, who must be grateful for something to do other than parodies of himself in Snickers commercials), who is picked up outside the gates of Statesville by his old partner Marv (Daniel Stern) in a scene reminiscent of the beginning of *The Blues Brothers*. Harry is still sore, physically and psychologically, from his past encounters with Kevin. He's also terminally ill with prostate cancer. As a final gift to a friend, Marv suggests that they return to the one house they couldn't successfully burgle, and the course is set for a collision between the squatter and the thieves.

The second third of the movie is basically a rehash of *Home Alone* and *Home Alone 2: Lost in New York*, but the elaborate traps and sadistic pranks feel tired this time around as Kevin and the Wet Bandits battle for control of the house. In a key moment, with Marv stuck in the kitchen window á la Pooh Bear and with Harry, clutching his groin, his hair singed and one hand stuck in a food processor, Kevin sinks to the floor and starts to sob. He admits to the crooks his various failures. He never imagined that the high point in his life would have been besting them. Now they're clutching at straws and scrambling after crumbs. "How did everything go so wrong?" Kevin asks. Reminding us why he won an Academy Award, an amazingly tender Pesci finds a soul in Harry, who manages to somehow comfort Kevin while giving vent to a long-simmering rage. In *Home Alone: Repossessed*, it's not only criminals but also the children of the nineties who've been screwed over by the system.

In the final act, Kevin and the Bandits go to Chicago to take on the real crooks. It seems that the mayor (Alan Ruck, in a piece of inspired casting) has been getting cozy with corporate interests and large campaign donors at the expense of the citizens. Our heroes align themselves with some Occupy-like outfit and use the tried-and-true traps and tortures to expose the Mayor's malfeasance.

Home Alone grossed over $533 million and remains one of the most popular films of the 1990s, a decade that in retrospect seems more and more like a Golden Age. It would be nice to think that Hollywood would be attuned to how things have changed and offer up stories that help us to conceive of better futures rather than to long for unrecoverable pasts, but the movies have always trafficked in nostalgia, which requires less thought and brings in more receipts at the box office. Look for *Home Alone: Repossessed* to be the first in a wave of films that represent the 1990s as a paradise lost.

Case in point, just last week *Variety* reported that director Penny Marshall and star Tom Hanks have signed on for *Small*, which involves a now middle-aged and morose Josh Baskin searching for a magical Zoltan machine to make him a little boy once more.

PHIL KIM

THE KARATE KID PREQUEL

Directed by Lars von Trier.

MOST CRITICS DISMISS SEQUELS and prequels as vehicles of basic financial prostitution, and in the past, the *Karate Kid* franchise has been no exception. While there are those who are quick to remind us that Pat Morita was originally nominated for an Academy Award for the first film of the series, there are countless others who pan the latter three or four films (depending on whether or not you view the Miyagi-less Smith/Chan product as a true sequel as some *KK* purists do not) as overly commodified garbage. But now this ferocious and oftentimes literally bloody, debate has been settled once and for all by the newest installment in the series, a prequel this time, that focuses upon a teenaged Miyagi and his Polish student "Jerzy," who goes on to become the grandfather of the greatest cinematic villain of all time: Johnny Lawrence.

Johnny Lawrence was played brilliantly in *KKI* by a young ingénue named William Zabka, and director/writer Lars von Trier blurs the fourth wall by naming his teenaged concentration camp prisoner protagonist "Jerzy Zabka." The choice of von Trier and his avant-garde Dogme 95 beliefs is in and of itself a bold demonstration of the film's producer Tyler Perry's commitment to resuscitate the overall artistic image of martial arts-based narratives. And von Trier's continued insistence upon raw filmmaking techniques and banishment of non-diegetic production actually works seamlessly in this tale that interweaves the profound and often simple philosophies of the martial arts into the inspirational story of the systematic murdering of millions of Jews.

Several of the sequels in the *KK* franchise begin with the same jumping-off point: the end of the All Valley Karate Tournament in which Daniel has beaten Johnny Lawrence. For example, *KKII* begins with Miyagi rescuing Johnny from his abusive sensei, who is infuriated that his pupil has lost to the skinny Italian kid from New Jersey and is disciplining Johnny in front of all of the other Cobra Kai. Or the third film, which focuses upon the aforementioned abusive sensei as the primary antagonist, and which also begins immediately after Johnny's defeat at All Valley and chronicles the sensei's immediate downfall. While von Trier's insistence upon a singular narrative timeframe without flashbacks or flashforwards may seem to have made this structural conceit inherently impossible, he ingeniously begins his own film with a scene that still thematically creates this overlap. In the scene, several prisoners at Sobibor argue over a piece of bread that one of them has smuggled from the kitchen. The actors in this scene are played by the entire original cast of actors that played the members of the Cobra Kai, including a now middle-aged William Zabka, Ron "Sweep the Leg" Thomas, Rob "Get Him a Bodybag" Garrison, and Martin Kove, who played the sensei. The ensuing result is both emotionally and metaphorically jarring and, oddly enough, a totally appropriate way to begin a martial arts movie.

After losing the fight for the piece of bread in the opening of the film, young Jerzy (played by Ryan Gosling) finds out that he and his mother are being transferred from Sobibor to Auschwitz. Jerzy's mother (Björk) is a deaf-mute camp prostitute whose vagina is slowly growing closed shut due to a rare genetic disorder. Her son Jerzy has inherited the male version of the same disease, so his mother has been saving her rations of soup and bread for the last three years in order to pay for an underground surgery to open up her son's shrinking penis hole permanently. But no one knows of her secret, not even Jerzy, and their transfer to Auschwitz has effectively ruined all of her preparations.

Jerzy and his mother go reluctantly to Auschwitz, where Jerzy can't seem to avoid trouble, both with the Germans and his fellow prisoners alike. His main tormentors are an entire group of his bunkmates, a gang known around the camp as the Kosher Kai, who use their advanced Krav Magra moves to humiliate him in front of all of the other prisoners during their Halloween dance parties and beach bonfires. In one particularly brutal scene, the boys in the Kosher Kai strip all of their clothes off before going to hunt Jerzy down, thus resembling a starved-down gang of martial-arts skeletons. As they close in on Jerzy, an eighteen-year-old Miyagi emerges from behind a barbed wire fence, and although his karate moves are somewhat slow and incredibly stiff, he magically defeats all of the Kosher Kai, who are depicted by actual officers in the Israeli army and Mossad. Jerzy and Miyagi slip away completely unharmed, and Miyagi leads them to the Zen garden that he has been secretly making inside of an unused gas chamber. Over green tea and sushi, Miyagi tells Jerzy of his background, of growing up in Okinawa and coming over to Poland along with a battalion of Japanese soldiers in support of the Third Reich.

He tells Jerzy how almost his entire battalion was raped and murdered by their German allies on their first night in Poland, and how he and the few other survivors were immediately shipped off to various work and death camps. Miyagi, who is currently Auschwitz's handyman, tells Jerzy all of this in near-perfect Polish, and von Trier's decision to not include English translations through subtitles, while baffling at first, does seem to further maintain the film's authenticity. Also, von Trier's decision to alter Miyagi's background, whom we know from the previous films to have come to America and joined the American army during World War II, seems to be a further commitment to making more complex and often morally conflicted main characters. Some critics have gone so far as to posit von Trier's new view of Miyagi as being akin to Batman's transition from comic books to the Dark Knight of the graphic novels.

After auditioning thousands of Asian American and Asian actors for the role of young Miyagi, the producers of the film made the controversial decision (despite the vehement objections by von Trier) to digitally create the character of Miyagi, combining the technology used for the film *Avatar* and for the Gollum character in the *Lord of the Rings* series. Martial arts legend Steven Seagal dons a special effects green suit to portray the physical movements of Miyagi, while actor Hank Azaria does his voice, and although it goes completely against his Dogme 95 aesthetic, the director has now conceded that digitally creating the character was the only real logical choice. Von Trier states, "Because we couldn't find a good half-Asian actor, we figured in the end that special effects were still preferable to casting a full-Asian type of Asian, which would not have been as believable." And the moody, morally complex Jerzy is played so perfectly by Gosling that we immediately forget all the controversy surrounding the digital Miyagi. And while some online sources have accused Gosling and his management team of deliberately choosing a role to offset his portrayal of a young neo-Nazi in *The Believer*, von Trier has come out personally to state that he cast Gosling because of the actor's "Semitic bone structure. Also, Ryan seems to be very good with money," the director has said, "which seemed realistic to me. Also, I believe that Hitler, if I were to step into his shoes for a little bit, would have hated a person that looked like Ryan, or people like Ryan. I don't know why, probably because of the size and shape of their noses, but I don't really know, I am just trying to empathize with a misunderstood man here, because that is how you get to the ultimate truth."

The film culminates the only way that martial arts movies should ever culminate: a fighting tournament. Miyagi, who has been dutifully training Jerzy by embedding karate techniques that normally take a lifetime to master into such mundane tasks as digging mass graves, painting tanks of Zyklon gas, skinning corpses, and waxing U-Boats, has signed Jerzy up for this year's All Auschwitz Tournament. There are a few surprising and welcome cameo appearances at the tournament, including Ralph Macchio as Primo Levi, Peter Dinklage as Elias the Dwarf, and Woody Allen as himself. While this critic won't reveal the film's overall and extremely surprising teleology, I will say that the conclusion is much more *Rocky I* than *Rocky V*. And I will also say that the numerous rape scenes throughout the film could have probably been boiled down to one or possibly even two rape scenes, or maybe even just a brief rape montage to get the point across, but again, I understand that it's all about realism and truth here. This *Karate Kid* prequel has changed my perception and emotional expectations for martial arts films, and will undoubtedly inform my future choices in life, should I ever find myself interned in an infamous Nazi concentration camp.

JOSH DUBOSE

CHARLY

Directed by Gus Van Sant. Written by Dustin Lance Black. Produced by Harvey Weinstein. Starring: Jake Gyllenhaal, Maggie Gyllenhaal, Ben Kingsley, and Christina Applegate.

WITH MOST FILMMAKERS THESE days referencing seventies cinema—films like *Dog Day Afternoon, Network, The Deer Hunter*—as the height of American filmmaking, a time when a director made a movie and not the studio, it comes as no surprise that a filmmaker with the caliber of Gus Van Sant has remade *Charly*, the 1968 adaptation of the novel *Flowers For Algernon* by Daniel Keyes.

"When the Weinsteins brought me the script I'd just wrapped *Milk* and was exhausted," said Van Sant. "I had no intention of taking on another project at the time even if Dustin [Lance Black] had written it. I had tears in my eyes by page three. Then Harvey [Weinstein] told me that Maggie and Jake [Gyllenhaal] were attached as the love interests…and…I wept again."

In a role that won Cliff Robertson an Academy Award, Jake Gyllenhaal boldly portrays Charly Gordon, a mentally disabled man who undergoes an experimental surgery designed to make him normal. After the procedure, Charly awakens to the world around him, gaining an understanding he'd been unable to attain before, and at the same time grappling with more complex emotional equations.

"It was an incredible challenge to act retarded," says Jake Gyllenhaal. "And then to switch and pretend to be really smart. There are so many levels to the mentally disabled and the super intelligent. I'd be lying if I said I wasn't intimidated…but I did a lot of research. I volunteered at a special-needs camp and realized that they face complex life situations. It's not all crayons and waffle cones like some people think."

Charly's tutor, Alice Kinnian, played so gracefully by Maggie Gyllenhaal, realizes Charly is surpassing the doctor's wildest expectations and becoming a genius, while at the same time trying to deny her blossoming feelings for an increasingly attentive Charly. When she refuses his initial advances, Charly tours the country on a motorcycle. Here, Van Sant captures the majestic American landscape beautifully and manages to layer the scenes with the political underpinnings of intolerance, all through Charly's eyes.

Charly's passion-filled return to Alice instantly puts this film into cinematic history. The starkly lit, tear-stained love scenes are some of the most haunting visuals ever caught on celluloid and will surely catch the attention of the Academy in the film's late-year release.

At the press tour in New York, Maggie had this to say: "What we had to do was shed our brother/sister identities, our familial ties, rise above them so to speak. Gus was very patient with us [she laughs] in rehearsals and on set. He was very kind and let us explore the nature of these characters, the subtle intricacies of this relationship for however long we needed."

Dr. Richard Nemur (Sir Ben Kingsley) and Dr. Anna Straus (Christina Applegate) track Charly's progress post-surgery and are exhilarated by the implications of the surgery's success until it's noticed that Algernon, the laboratory mouse and original recipient of the experimental procedure, is regressing, losing his ability to complete even simple mazes and slowly grows more retarded than he'd been before. Nemur and Straus are now left, along with the film's viewers, to wonder what will become of Charly Gordon and Alice Kinnian as their story continues to unfold.

Van Sant successfully kept this project from the public eye by shooting all the interiors at Leavesden Studios in London and using both Maggie and Jake on location only one time.

"We had to shoot for Central Park. So, we talked to the London Film Commission and were able to block off almost six acres in Thames Chase Park for the picnic scene. It was quite a feat. We just didn't want people judging the film before we had the chance to present it in the proper context," said Van Sant. In addition, only Sir Ben Kingsley was privy to the fact that the brother and sister duo were the leads as he had several scenes with the both of them.

"When I saw the film," said Applegate, "I was floored. It's truly beautiful. But they should've told me. I mean, I wouldn't have said anything."

Critics and moviegoers will be talking about this film for years to come. The Gyllenhaals' transformation into these characters, as well as their onscreen chemistry, is so spellbinding that one's initial fears and expectations are set aside once the film begins to roll. *Charly* is a triumph over taboos.

JIM SHEPARD

THREE FILMS

Abbott and Costello Meet the Bankers (1949)

Coming just a year on the heels of the considerable box-office success of their lash-up with the Universal monsters in *Abbott and Costello Meet Frankenstein* and employing much of the same cast, this late A&C vehicle featured some memorably grotesque imagery and low comedy, but its unexpectedly apocalyptic ending—featuring the collapse of the world economy and the boys' decision, having been marooned at sea, to eat the stowaway they find cowering in their lifeboat, *Pillage Today* magazine editor Waldo Whinesecker (Vincent Price)—pretty much insured the end of Universal's attempts at a Boys-Meet-the-Monsters cycle.

The world of Wall Street messengers Herbie Broadhurst (Lou Costello) and Chick Young (Bud Abbott) is turned topsy-turvy when Haldex Fisting, the president of the US Bank of the Republic (Bela Lugosi), in league with the craven and zoophagous head of the Federal Reserve J. Roscoe Eck (Dwight Frye, in a performance that makes even his Renfield in 1931's *Dracula* seem the very model of comportment and dignity), hatch a plot to secretly dump the Bank's toxic derivatives into a taxpayer-insured subsidiary.

With Glenn Strange, Lon Chaney Jr. and Lavrentiy Beria (!) in a rare cameo as the Secretary of the Treasury.

The Five Obstructions (2012)

Provocateur Lars von Trier's remake of his own semi-documentary *The Five Obstructions* from 2003, with the same premise, features his mischievous dare that five of the Justices of the United States Supreme Court are to attempt, in various ways that he has stipulated, to dismantle American democracy. With James Woods as John Roberts, John Lithgow as Anthony Kennedy, Kevin Pollack as Samuel Alito, Roseanne Barr as Antonin Scalia, and Robert Downey Jr. as Clarence Thomas.

20,000 Years in Sing Sing (2014)

Jim Carrey's searing remake of Michael Curtiz's 1933 classic about unjust incarceration, with Tom Hanks as the history high school teacher/Little League coach turned hardened criminal after having spent forty-five years in prison, having been sentenced for attending a rally in support of the right to rally under the terms of President Obama's new NDAA law allowing the indefinite detention of American citizens. With both Rooney Mara and Helen Mirren as his heartbroken and long-suffering wife (Mara when he goes in, and Mirren when he comes out) and Rahm Emmanuel in his Academy Award-winning and legendarily persuasive turn as the smoothly charming and heartless warden.

LEN SHNEYDER

THE BEAT GENERATION

Directed by Curtis Hanson. Starring: Jamie Foxx, Owen Wilson, Adam Goldberg, and Will Smith as Allen Ginsberg. Inspired by Kerouac: A Biography by Ann Charters.

Anne Charters asked Kerouac a simple question: "What do you think about *On The Road*?" To which he replied: "I spent half my life writing *On The Road* and the other half living it down." Simply put: no one took Kerouac or anything he wrote as seriously after achieving such success so early in his career. The power of Curtis Hanson's new film is the tribute he pays to not only the author of *On The Road* but the legions of wayward souls that read it and found solace in what they perceived as the "story of their lives"; however, this isn't the core of Hanson's film. On the contrary, *On The Road*, and the actual road trip(s) that spawned the novel, are only window dressing into the layered complexities of Sal Paradise himself.

The camera pulls back from the side of the road and pans across the green leaves of corn stalks standing erect in the Midwest as a 1945 Buick roars past them. We're now in the passenger seat with two of the most iconic figures of postwar beatdown America: Jack Kerouac (Jamie Foxx) and his accomplice Neal Cassady (Owen Wilson). The car is roaring with two young men who embody, like this film, all that was wrong in a time when the world was recovering from World War II but at the same time embody and represent youth, beauty, and what's ever-present and possible in the human condition. But Foxx and Wilson aren't really part of America; their dialogue is concerned with Schopenhauer and the thing in and of itself being this or that sign or signifier. They are roaring through the backbone of the American breadbasket but their minds are strolling the gardens of the Buddha while their bodies could be temples to either Venus or Apollo. Hanson maneuvers his characters through a world that should be familiar, is familiar, but at the same time is a disjointed homage to the program and aesthetic of what later becomes the beatnik movement. The beats were not musicians in the sense that a beatnik wandered the world with bongos, a necklace of wooden and ceramic beads, and a soulpatch. No, a beatnik had been beaten down and the smack dab that Hanson performs on his audience is a dissociative one that splits viewer from familiarity of location and casts an audience en masse into disenfranchisement. Even though the diners "on the road" are as familiar as the apple pie served in them, the conversation and the personalities, scrolls of paper, Benzedrine binges in which Foxx hunches over his Underwood typing at a frenetic pace—they approach the beatitude of a saint from another era that's altogether foreign to the landscape of America and presents the audience with a fundamental question to answer: Whose America is this?

Even though Foxx wasn't a natural fit for the role of Jack Kerouac, he brings to the film a certain natural dislocation and disenfranchisement (don't repeat this word) that from the first scene marks him like Cain. No one ever questions that Foxx is meant to stay at the Docks in San Francisco, or that any decision he makes is truly his own. Quite the contrary, the more Foxx's Kerouac rebels against what appears normal, and/or sane, the more we cheer and find ourselves in need of a personal and profound revolution—violence of course is optional.

This cross-country trip is ultimately trumped as Kerouac falls into the circle of miscreants and social pariahs called artists until the spectacled king and high priest of Doric romance walks out of a bathroom in a Soho loft party amid a cloud of smoke so thick a ghost would feel lost: Allen Ginsberg. Ginsberg (Will Smith) is immediately attracted to Jack, who stands bridging the world of the American male and the nineteenth-century dandy, a gruff blue-collar exterior with a gentle and honed sense of beauty within. Smith floats like Balanchine to the side of Kerouac and without any great surprise or heavy-handed profundity says. "Cigarette?"

The offer of a fag between the two men hangs as thick as caramel in the air; Foxx and Smith, their eyes locked in a duel like Ice and Bernardo, until they drop their ocular knives as recognition takes hold and the word "brother" manifests in the sugar between them.

But we know all to well what's too come amidst New York hipsters: the scene is thick with binge-drinking and benny-popping that fuels intelligentsia and its love affair with itself—but that's not the only love afoot. It's no great secret that Ginsberg's affection for boys wasn't restricted to those younger than him, but rather after his return from India and an obvious tussle among street urchins he sets his crosshairs on a slowly eroding Jack.

The late fifties weren't kind to Kerouac, who suffered both physically and spiritually, finding himself a kind of joke among those that went on the road and then got off of it—opting instead to sire their children in the booming suburbs. Jack is a fossil, a remnant of the past, while Ginsberg has evolved into the icon of tomorrow, not only adopting the West's appetite for Eastern spirituality but living it, on his sleeve. The meeting and the familiarity it spawns is a tender moment in the film where a has-been tells the soon-to-be of the troubles that come from climbing high and fast. Smith's is a veritable bodhisattva of compassion as he watches and listens to Foxx's pain and lamentation. The pain isn't simply his bitterness, but that of an entire generation of second-class artists who would only be acknowledged as such many years later in their university and café canonizations. But what the audience realizes, and Foxx in all his erudition is completely aware of, is that that's how it is, how it's meant to be. Only rock stars find instant fame and glory in their own age; the other arts wait for death to pitch them forward to the stars. Foxx finishes with the words, "How's a man like me to be loved who can never learn to love being a man like me?" To which Smith replies calmly and coolly, "Jack, I love you. Don't you know that I've always loved you?! Jack, I'll blow you."

The film could end here, but Hanson takes it all the way to the deathbed of Ginsberg, who is remembering his many loves, writing his last poems, and fondling a small daisy. As his mind wanders and he recalls the summer of '69 when the world changed into a world where Kerouac was no longer a part of it, the pain written on his face and twitching beard is not for his loss, but our loss. Smith makes us believe in a few short minutes before his own passing that his world isn't complete without Foxx, that when he lost Foxx we all lost a piece of the true America, the diner mystic, the gas station saint, the yeoman magician, all of these magical creatures that will forever be immortalized for us, on the road.

Hanson brings down the house quietly through Ginsberg, who lived like a titan through some of the most tumultuous decades firmly rooted in America's psyche of itself. What we are left with is neither satisfaction that we revere Kerouac nor acceptance that Ginsberg and his flawed volumes of poems are the gems of "Kaddish" and "Howl," no; Hanson leaves us uncertain of our own surroundings and the world we inhabit. It won't matter if you see the film in Duluth, Minnesota, New York or Bahrain: the effect is the same—this is the America of a 1950s imagination soaked in the kerosene of Eastern philosophy.

SHIRIN NAJAFI

THE BOOB SWITCH

Directed by David Dobkin. Starring: Ryan Reynolds, Jason Sudeikis, Isla Fisher, and Keira Knightley.

JUST WHEN IT SEEMED Hollywood couldn't outdo itself with a premise devoid of any merit—save for its ability to be pitched to a movie exec with an anxiety disorder—along comes this comedy from the creators of other comedies whose names and storylines you've forgotten even though you're pretty sure you saw them in the theater or on Netflix or on a movie channel like HBO.

The Boob Switch, as the title suggests, is about two men whose wives switch boob sizes. It begins with an introduction to the lives of two couples who live in a generic suburb outside of an unnamed city that is probably Chicago. Dave (Ryan Reynolds) works in advertising and is married to the voluptuous Krissy (Isla Fisher), a food critic. Steve (Jason Sudeikis) has a job in finance and is married to the lithe and flat-chested Carolyn (Keira Knightley), a yoga instructor.

In the film's pivotal scene, Dave and Steve meet for a drink at a bar. The evening starts as a regular night between two friends, catching up and complaining. As the two become drunker, the complaining extends to their love lives. Dave, who spends his days looking at glossy advertising photos of women, wishes his wife had a more svelte figure. Steve, on the other hand, feels that his wife Carolyn is becoming thinner and thinner and her breasts have virtually disappeared. It becomes evident that each man vies for the physical body—specifically breast size—of the other's wife. At this moment, a toothless Irish bartender mutters under his breath, "Careful what you wish for," before crushing up a bunch of four-leaf clovers and sprinkling lucky clover dust into their next round of drinks.

After the men go home, a lightning storm strikes. Whether this lightning is induced by the four-leaf clover dust or is just a perfect coincidence (and a necessary second component to the spell that is to ensue later) is unclear. We see the respective couples asleep in bed as the lightning cascades into their bedrooms, causing them to toss and turn in the presumed discomfort of the impending physical and psychological metamorphoses.

The next morning, as was promised by the movie poster, Carolyn the yoga instructor has double Ds, and Krissy, the once-voluptuous food critic, has double As. Here, the film takes pains to clarify certain rules of this new universe. Apparently no one can see this change in breast size except for the two husbands. We learn this when Krissy, who now looks flat-chested, dresses herself and looks in a mirror completely unfazed.

She meets a friend for lunch who compliments her on her curvy figure and the fact that she can really fill out a dress.

The inherent comedy in all this is heightened when Carolyn, the day after her transformation, goes bra shopping. She walks into a Victoria's Secret with double Ds and asks where she can find a "training bra" because As are now too big for her. The salesperson unflinchingly walks her to the teenage section of the store, and we watch as Keira Knightley hilariously holds up a training bra to her double D boobs in a mirror.

Despite the film's exhausting effort to clarify the rules of this universe, the viewer must still make a few leaps of faith—especially in terms of spatiality. How does Knightley fit the training bra over her double Ds? When Steve is excitedly massaging the breasts of his newly voluptuous wife, does she see his hand moving at an eight-inch distance from her chest?

Dave and Steve, of course, freak out the morning they wake up to their transformed wives. They remain calm until they get into their cars going to work and call each other. "My wife has boobs!" / "My wife has no boobs!" they simultaneously exclaim. In a state of confusion and madness, Dave slams his steering wheel,

"Dude, what happened?" Steve, meanwhile, tries to see the bright side: "You know, maybe this isn't a bad thing after all?" One has to wonder if Steve's attitude is inspired by the fact that he's getting the better end of the deal: his wife is rail thin with enormous boobs while Dave's wife is stout with no boobs. Regardless, he convinces Dave, and the two happily enjoy this new transformation. A series of hilarious boob-themed antics ensue from approximately minute twenty-five to minute fifty-five of the film.

Ultimately, the men realize they need to undo the spell and return to the original breast sizes of their wives. Here, we discover that behind this inane comedy is actually a heartfelt message: love is blind. Or, maybe love is irrespective of breast size. Whatever it is, it's a compelling message that fills you with the most minimal sense of fulfillment and prevents you from asking for your money back at the end of the film (or smashing the DVD box into a wall if watching from home).

The men orchestrate a "girls' night" for their wives so that they can meet alone in one of their homes, as it would be too easy to just meet somewhere else. They pace around a living room decorated with furniture from Pottery Barn, jotting various ideas on a paper easel with the heading "Boob Switch." Just when it seems they've exhausted absolutely every idea, Steve realizes that they should just retrace their steps the night before the boob switch happened. Except instead of complaining about their wives' breast sizes, they should praise them.

Accordingly, the two men return to the bar and execute the plan. The toothless bartender knowingly smiles, as if having taught these two men a lesson, and crushes up a reverse four-leaf clover potion and puts it into their drinks. Thunder and lightning strike, and the men wake up the following morning to their wives in their original physical states.

The last five minutes of the film are dedicated to a period of "happily ever after" that seems to continually outdo itself in happily-ever after-ness. The men, who wake in blissful peace next to their wives, decide to organize a "wife appreciation dinner." It's set up in one of their backyards, where the table is lit with candles and surrounded by paper lanterns. At dinner, each man confesses what he loves most about his wife, both physically and emotionally. The wives are touched by the display before deciding to crack a few crass and out-of-place one-liners to jolt us out of the seriousness of the conversation. The men officially declare this day as "Wife Appreciation Day," given that such a day doesn't exist—only Mother's Day, which doesn't count for couples without children. A fun song plays, as we zoom out of the Chicago suburbs and watch as this backyard becomes a tiny microcosm of a greater world with other families and marriages. Credits begin to roll as you get up from your chair and slowly begin the process of forgetting whether you ever saw this film.

RYAN WILSON

WHEEL OF TRUTH

Directed by Pat Sajak. Starring: Pat Sajak.

FLASH FORWARD ONE HUNDRED years, five hundred years—hell, let's turn it up to one thousand—to the archival system of our culture, viewable in the retinas of what passes for humans, the AI-infused beings that inhabit not Earth exactly but a kind of virtual landscape that contains elements of physical reality: dirt, the occasional tree, streets, structures, but really, "the world" is more of a suspended post-digital, synaptical time-space field controlled by the programming of the creators.

Or something.

What are the films of our era that will live on? There are only two options:

1. The most vapid of Hollywood superhero-explosion-terrorist-redemption.

2. The personal documentary.

Though I have to psych myself up sometimes before engaging this sometimes/often self-regarding genre, this is where I'd put my longevity money. These are the only stories that our future relatives will scour, full of artificial curiosity, *why, why are these poor hairless chimpanzees trying to piece together meaning out of what they called life?*

Why indeed.

As an unabashed gameshow fanatic in my fructose youth, the most repellent of all of the combed-over fiends was unquestionably The Sajak. Both smug and insipid, condescending without a shred of a reason to be, and fearless—utterly fearless—to look America straight in the eye with a joke that (he knows) contains zero value of any perceptible kind, Sajak clearly possessed the coveted personality pieces to climb Olympus, and so his rise must have felt, to him, inevitable, determined, as if he'd pulled the sword from the stone.

Wheel of Truth debuted at the 4-H Branson Film Festival this year to an audience paralyzed by a combination of shock and instant transcendence. There were no walk-outs. There were *no sounds*. No sniffles, popcorn crunches, chair squeaks—there was only stillness and rapt attention. What emerges from the first frame is a New Poetry, a visual immediacy and intimacy, with Sajak's voice (now heavily weathered by a lake of Scotch and quarry of Pall Malls) ringing out in ninety-second bursts of a kind of melding between the profane and sacred that could only be wrought from a soul that had spun itself into oblivion, thinning with each turn of random commerce.

In the opening shot the camera moves achingly slow, almost indiscernibly—closer and closer to the Wheel, as the clicky thing finally stops on "Jamaica." Sajak takes us straight to the face of a seventy-five-year-old white woman, the winner, exultant, coming out of her skin. And then... he speaks:

> *That trip to Jamaica, the Dunn's River Falls all the souls squeezing into one another, palm to palm (holy palmer's kiss)*
>
> *ascending against the stream of paradise—the wheel found you, took you there*
>
> *and you looked it in the eyes, haggling for a piece of shit on the street,*
>
> *a boat made of shells, five dollar! she demands. And you say, no, one dollar! Because it is your money, your dollar, your world, your God.*

The film references some of the visual language of Russ McElwee's *Sherman's March* and, more recently, Sarah Polley's excellent *Stories We Tell*. While I believe both of those gems will live on indefinitely in the mostly horrible future, what Sajak has

done here is to use these personal docs as a jumping-off point, the
way Dylan began with Guthrie and Muddy Waters, only later to
explode at Newport. This film is a detonator.

Imagine the beautiful Los Angeles morning, Sajak with an
Americano in hand, striding in his loafers into the heart of Merv
Griffin's operation. *I want to make a documentary, kind of a special
really, about the Wheel. The big jackpots. The bankruptcies. The
celebratory gyrating. Talk to the winners now. Vanna, of course.
Rural Wisconsin. Michigan. Ohio. Kentucky. Alabama. They'd eat it
up. Life on the Wheel, something like that.*

Okay, Pat. Sounds like a real champ. How's five million sound?

Sajak's evolutionary artistic middle as a meaningful figure
in right-wing punditry and fund-raising must have given the
bosses every reason to believe he'd churn out a piece of puffery so
undeniable it could choke a child, as if filled with a load of taffy,
M&Ms, and bleach. Pure gold. What I long to see, and never will,
is the pivot Sajak must have made, like a ballerina, out the doors
of Griffin's office, knowing he'd just walked away clean, with their
unwitting blessing to make a film about the great, unspeakable
emptiness in our credit-card hearts.

Where other personal docs might glorify the fleeting moments
we spend with a very young Sajak (DJ'ing his way to early fame,
then to Vietnam, his time with Armed Forces Radio), Sajak slams
the door on any such maudlin inclinations. The footage of Sajak
accidentally pulling the plug on Nixon's 1969 broadcast to the
troops only serves the film's greater purpose of exposing its own
subject as a mindless noise in a sea of cacophony. Again, though,
Sajak refuses to stop here, with simple irony. He pushes us further
down the river, to the level of reality behind what beams into our
homes. Try this voiceover on for size as the camera zeroes in on
his own eyes, caught mid-laugh as he fumbles with the old Army
radio equipment:

Napalm and the beast that laps it up the milk of war

Lockheed Martin, Boeing, Bell, General Dynamics
only now can I hear the murder in the names,

now that there are no stakes, no meaning,

names that simply float on the billions becoming
trillions becoming meaningless sound

meaningless value, human life

the sound of my voice, what I mean (nothing) what
I say to you now, this instant

an agent of the dream that weakens us.

In what would have to qualify as further evidence that the Jungian model of the Collective Unconscious indeed makes itself manifest at the time of a great shared experience, I could hear in the theater two hundred near whispers, all forming the same letters: V-A-N-N-A W-H-I-T-E. After the initial plunge into Sajak's agonizing world, after he exposes us (and himself) to his fatalist poetic commentary, we are left as viewers wondering at what point in his opus will he give us the face, the hands, the legs walking the horizontal plane, as if her only purpose, her only knowledge, contained the twenty-six letters, that, when flipped, turned beggars into kings.

SPOILER ALERT

One of the truths about human nature that Sajak exploits throughout *Wheel* is our need to visually orient ourselves each second. Against the spiral of dollar signs and traps, we hear the legendary announcer Charly O'Donnell echo from beyond... *Pat Sajak and Vanna White!*

Sajak hard cuts to himself and Vanna, present day, their faces only inches apart. Our eyes scramble to make sense of them seated on two folding chairs in a women's bathroom, a toilet in plain view.

The following are snippets from the interview—or more accurately,
their exchange of souls.

> *Vanna, remember when the fat man in suspenders
> fell onto the wheel, and I looked at you, and you
> ran over from the puzzle to get a closer look, and
> everyone thought you were trying to help him?*

> *Oh yes. And I looked back at you, and I realized I'd
> been so blessed to have you there every day.*

> *Those were the words I made you say before work,
> over coffee and ratings, in this bathroom.*

> *And…*

> *What is waking up like for you these days, Vanna?
> Walk me through it.*

> *I roll right out of bed and beat a punching bag for
> five minutes. I drink breakfast and work out for
> four hours. Then it's time for my face.*

> *I'd like to start having you over for tea, just you and
> me, every Sunday. How would you like that?*

The audience was brought to whatever tears they had left in
their stricken faces. How I ended up on the panel of the Branson
Film Festival is, perhaps, a story for another time (RIP. Ned Beatty).
The Christian Vegas, though, made for a perfectly unironic setting
for the unveiling of art. For a tight seventy-eight minutes, Sajak
takes us down the river until we finally reach his own personal
Kurtz, his ill-fated talk show, the absolute apex of vacancy beamed
into American homes. But the journey to the bottom of this pit
is worth every strained second—because, truly, how many times
in life does one have the great *fortune* to bear witness to the birth
of the pure artist? Especially the miraculous, rare December
bloom, in the face of long odds, when the Wheel lands squarely on
Bankrupt, and never before now has that felt like such a jackpot.

SUMMER BLOCK

THE MIDDLE MAN

Directed by Steven Soderbergh. Written by Jason Reitman. Starring: George Clooney, Matt Damon, Rachel Weisz, and Tilda Swinton.

PLEASE FORGIVE ANY TYPOS that may appear in this review, but I just walked out of *The Middle Man* two hours ago and my hands are still shaking! How can I even begin to describe the experience of seeing *The Middle Man* on the big screen? Well, for starters, there was the screen. It is a *big* screen. Like, incredibly huge. I mean, I went into it knowing that it was going to be a big screen, bigger certainly than a cellphone screen or an iPad screen or even most average home television screens. But nothing prepared me for this! Imagine the biggest TV you've ever seen in your entire life—this is like a hundred times bigger than that! And if that's not enough, it's flanked with these gorgeous red velvet curtains with all these luxuriant drapes and folds—and you have to picture these curtains are like thirty feet long, so we're talking about maybe ten yards of fabric here, per curtain, so that's maybe $2,000 worth of velvet, just for the curtains. And worth every penny, trust me.

As you might expect, I watched *The Middle Man* while seated. But I wasn't sitting in a straight-backed chair or on a rough-hewn bench, I can tell you that! No, here's where *The Middle Man* really delivered, with plush, oversize seats that actually reclined. Fear not, penny-pinchers: the fold-down armrests are included in the price of the ticket!

A word of warning: the theater is quite dark. It's much darker than the average person keeps their living room, even when viewing films at home, and it's certainly much darker than pretty much any other commonly frequented public space. Be advised to move safely around the theater and to keep aisles clear at all times.

Now I know what you're thinking—she's raved about the screens, the curtains, the seats (and did I mention they have snacks?!) but what about the film itself? Readers, I'm glad you asked. *The Middle Man* was simply astounding. The sparkling dialogue alone was more than worth the price of admission. I don't know about you, but whenever I have conversations with my friends, there are plenty of "likes" and "ums" and awkward pauses, and most of the time even when we do get the words out right, all we're really saying is boring stuff about our jobs and our insurance premiums and what is or is not affecting our seasonal allergies. But pretty much every word that was said by any character in *The Middle Man* was clever and important, and delivered so clearly, too, just incredibly sharp and witty and well-enunciated. Whenever anyone insulted someone else, or made a sexual innuendo or a veiled threat, the other person would immediately respond with something just completely *apropos* and off-the-cuff. I wish my friends were like that!

And, while it may be unprofessional to say so, may I add that the actors delivering the lines were all very good-looking? Sure, sometimes they might have appeared disheveled or drunken or bloodied or dead, but even then, they were somehow still quite good-looking. I know it sounds unrealistic, but somehow, when it's on that giant screen, you totally buy it.

But trust me, *The Middle Man* is not all talk—it's also nonstop action! Do you know how in your daily life, a lot of things just sort of happen but don't really lead anywhere? Like, maybe you meet your future wife, and you fall in love, and you get married, but in between you also buy a bird and get your oil changed and have strep throat and watch *Hoarders*? *The Middle Man* is nothing like that. Every single scene is a meaningful part of the main character's life, from graduating law school to finding his fiancée mysteriously poisoned to hijacking a chartered plane. Even things that seem sort of trivial and meaningless at first, like the main character stopping to give a dollar to a panhandler on the subway platform—spoiler alert!—turns out to have an important meaning in the end. There's also music playing all the time, which sounds distracting but it isn't—in fact, the mood of the music perfectly complements the mood of the scene.

And the sound! It's very loud, but also very clear, like sitting inside a giant silver bell.

In conclusion, *The Middle Man* is a can't-miss film. The only thing that could possibly have made it better would be if it were somehow possible to view it with an additional dimension, but of course, that would be absurd.

SOFIYA ALEXANDRA

BOSOM BROS 8: BROS 4 LIFE

Directed by Michael Bay. Starring: Dwayne Johnson, Vin Diesel, Bruce Willis, Channing Tatum, Jessica Alba, and Tyrese Gibson.

LET ME JUST START this review by saying WOW. I mean WOW!!! I had heard a lot of hype about this movie, mostly from Gavin, my sister's husband, who's rad to the max and drives a Porsche his work gave him, so I was pretty worried there was no way for this movie to live up to all these expectations! But guess what?? If you're talking the recipe for a perfect blockbuster, amigo, you've found it! There's hot chicks, cars, explosions, hot chicks, bad guys, and did I mention the hot chicks??? I had no idea it was going to be so good, and now I am kicking myself for not splurging on the Blu-ray right away, but honestly I don't mind having two copies of this movie because you can never have too much awesome. I literally got on Amazon the minute it was over to try and preorder the 3-D version—it is that good. And it's like, you would think that you can't make eight movies about the same thing and have them be cool as hell the whole time, but you would be WRONG, muchacho.

I gotta admit, at first I was a little bit confused between all the male characters, The Rock, Willis, Vin Diesel, and Channing Tatum, because they are all real swole kickass dudes who are bald. But I rewound a bunch of times and I think I get it now. Basically, they are a crew of badass guys who are super-close like brothers even though they all have their own thing, like Bruce Willis is like an old Army guy, and Vin Diesel loves grapes, and The Rock is like secretly a painter and he's super good, and Channing has a huge dick. And they are all just living their lives until crime boss Tyrese does something to one of their cars, or Jessica Alba, I don't remember exactly because like RIGHT AWAY The Rock or Vin Diesel drives this sweet cherried-out Lambo INTO ANOTHER MOTHERFUCKING LAMBO, BOOM!!! I know. I literally couldn't believe how pumped I was after that stunt!! And that's just the beginning.

Because Tyrese hires a bunch of Chinese gangsters, one of whom is Harold or Kumar, whichever the Chinese one is, to kidnap Jessica Alba, who is married to The Rock or Bruce Willis or she is one of their daughters or something, I think maybe like one is her dad, but the other one is her husband, anyway. The next thing you know we're in Mexico and I guess Tyrese has like a cocaine farm there, and so BOOM all the bros jump out of a helicopter to land in Tyrese's cocaine field even though Channing or The Rock is real skeptical his wife/daughter is there and thinks it's a setup, but Vin Diesel is all like cracking super tough jokes and eating grapes so you feel like it's gonna be okay, then as they jump out, THE HELICOPTER CRASHES INTO THREE OTHER HELICOPTERS that Tyrese has circling the island of Mexico and shooting at the bros. Then, those helicopters explode, AND THE BLADE FROM ONE CUTS KUMAR OR HAROLD'S HEAD OFF and the second helicopter CRASHES INTO A MEXICAN VOLCANO which totally explodes lava and you see it DESTROY A WHOLE MOTHERFUCKING VILLAGE. At this point I switched to Diet Mountain Dew because for serious, my heart could not take the action!!

So even though the bros are like crazy tight, they still have disagreements, especially The Rock and Vin Diesel. The Rock is maybe the toughest of all the dudes, like if you're going bicep circumference or just overall swoleness or best tats, so he keeps how kickass he is at painting on the DL, and Vin Diesel starts accusing him of keeping secrets, and challenges him for leadership of the bros. Right away you can feel The Rock is mad ferosh in his role. Oooh man, I almost wanted to shout to Vin Diesel, don't do it, dude!! Don't get him mad!!!! But at the same time I'm like DO IT, THIS SHOWDOWN IS GONNA BE SO EPIC!!

Dudes, I don't wanna ruin anything for you, but guess what, THE FIGHT WAS SOOO BRUTAL!! It was like, FISTS, MOUTH, HEADLOCK, GUT PUNCHES, GETTING THROWN OFF A TOWER INTO THE MEXICAN OCEAN, UNDERWATER FIGHT WITH KNIVES, LEG SWEEPS, HEAD BUTTS, GETTING THROWN OFF A TALLER TOWER, GRENADE FIGHT, INSULTS ABOUT EACH OTHER'S BALLS, SCRATCHING, LASER FIGHT, USING HEAD AS BONGO DRUM, BLEEDING, COMING TO A REASONABLE RESOLUTION THROUGH THE WISE WORDS OF ARMY DUDE BRUCE WILLIS AND SEXY DANCING OF CHANNING TATUM. I mean, CLASSIC!! The bros make up and The Rock finally tells Vin about his painting and Vin of course doesn't make fun of him, how could The Rock ever think that, they are super-tight bros.

Oh so the thing I forgot was, Tyrese has Jessica Alba all pretending to be his girlfriend in this crazy awesome silver bikini and her boobs look HUUGE, like way bigger than in *Fantastic Four*, maybe cause she had a baby since then, whatever, the point is she looks crazy hot, I almost licked my TV lol sue me I'm a guy ;). So anyway Tyrese is basically screwing with the heads of the bros by like making Jessica Alba act like his girlfriend and like serve them drinks and wings and shit in that dope bikini while Tyrese is all kissing on her, to get The Dees and The Rock all heated and lose focus on their mission because COME ON it's their wife/daughter, and that shit is NOT cool. I was pretty surprised by Tyrese's performance, I thought he was just another bald ripped dude who looked great but he was legit creepy in this role and made me mad and Jessica Alba isn't even my wife/daughter, that's REAL acting, for all those haters out there. So the two bros are getting pretty pissed at Tyrese, and BAM they fall into his trap and suddenly there's SYLVESTER MOTHERFUCKING STALLONE!!!

At this point in the review if you shit yourself, it's totally understandable and no one would even blame you because WHAT A RAD SURPRISE. And he is just beating the bejesus out of the bros and it honestly seems like they aren't fighting back that much because HE IS A GODDAMN LEGEND LET HIM DO WHAT HE WANTS. They are definitely gonna lose with that kind of attitude because Stallone is a BEAST and he's aged really good like wine and Jessica Alba looks pretty worried because obviously who wants to screw Tyrese with his rapey eyes in this movie. BUT THEN out of nowhere, Bruce Willis and The Tate BURST THROUGH THE CEILING ON PARACHUTES and just surprise take down Tyrese and Stallone, who barely loses because he is awesome.

And Jessica Alba is so psyched she's not gonna get raped she totally frenches Diesel or Rock, whichever one is not her dad and then everyone drives Hummers into the sunset and they play Kid Rock AND I CANNOT BELIEVE THIS THRILL RIDE IS OVER.

The bottom line is I'm gonna miss all of the bros, Vin, B-Willy, Rocktacular, The Chan-Chan Man, the whole crew, but I will be forever thankful for the powerful memories, and also I have this movie in regular and Blu-ray and soon 3-D and I hear they're making BB 9 soon!!! Obviously, I highly recommend it, unless you're a total moron who read this and still doesn't want to see it, YOU ARE NOT WORTHY, IDIOT. Hope the rest of you guys love it like me, peace.

JOSHUA KORNREICH

WALT DISNEY'S 101 ONE-PERCENTERS

Directed by Martin Scorsese. Written by Aaron Sorkin. Starring: Johnny Depp, Bradley Cooper, Amy Adams, Leonardo DiCaprio, George Clooney, Brad Pitt, Matt Damon, Ben Affleck, Mark Wahlberg, Jeremy Renner, Ryan Gosling, Alec Baldwin, Matthew McConaughey, Adam Sandler, Ben Stiller, Owen Wilson, Vince Vaughn, Will Ferrell, Steve Carell, Paul Rudd, Ryan Reynolds, Seth Rogen, Jonah Hill, Tom Cruise, Tom Hanks, Robert De Niro, Morgan Freeman, etc., Mike Tyson, Ted. Executive Producers: All of the above.

So, is MARTIN SCORSESE's follow-up to *The Wolf of Wall Street* another indictment of the culture of excess or is it just another glorification of it? Well, that probably depends on whom you ask.

Walt Disney's 101 One-Percenters, a darkly humorous, often sophomoric take-off of the classic animated feature *Walt Disney's 101 Dalmatians*, stars every actor you've seen in every movie every year for the last twenty years. All the actors in this film, with few exceptions, are white, male, and in the guise of the lovable black-and-white spotted puppies. Yes, even roles usually reserved for animated canines are now physically being taken up by the wealthiest one percent of Hollywood heavyweights.

Johnny Depp lends his androgynously attractive features to yet another character role, this time the evil kidnapress Cruella de Vil. Once again, Depp infuses his character with the physical spasms of not a Rolling Stone but another rock legend: David Bowie. While this source of inspiration seems to work in certain scenes, in others, Depp comes off more like Rocky Horror's Dr. Frank N. Furter than Bowie's Ziggy Stardust.

Roger and Anita, the human father and mother figures to all the puppies, are played by Bradley Cooper and Amy Adams. Mr. Cooper continues to demonstrate his dramatic as well as comedic range despite certain distractions: namely, Robert De Niro. While it is on one level a real treat to see De Niro finally reunited with his longtime collaborator Mr. Scorsese, it is, at the same time, disturbing to see him involved in yet another Bradley Cooper vehicle. This troublesome sign is reinforced in several of their scenes together, as De Niro's canine character seems unable to control his urge to hump Cooper's leg whenever they're in the same shot. With this film under his belt, De Niro may have finally taken the crown from Michael Caine for never seeing a script he did not like. (Note: Perhaps in fear of his reputation being threatened, Mr. Caine has reportedly signed on as the butler for this movie's sequel, *Lee Daniels' 101 One-Percenters and Their Butler.*)

In another f-you to struggling actors everywhere who can never find enough roles to support an adequate living, Cruella's two henchmen are played by Ted (of *Ted* fame) and former heavyweight boxing champ turned stage thespian Mike Tyson. While this casting decision of pairing a stuffed animal with a convicted rapist might seem silly, and even repugnant to some audiences, it is hard to deny the dramatic intensity Tyson brings to the table whenever he chews off a hunk of Ted's ear or shoves him into the front of his trousers for firing insults at him regarding his genitalia. In fact, by the time all the puppies are rescued from the two thugs, Ted, no longer seen on screen, is only heard muttering "fuck," "shit," and "asshole," underneath Tyson's underpants.

For a reason never fully explained, the puppy played by Matthew McConaughey sits in the corner of the room for the whole film, pounding his chest awkwardly, refusing to eat, and wondering why the other puppies in the room find him utterly annoying.

Speaking of annoying, Adam Sandler, who also plays one of the puppies, strums the folk guitar and makes weird and irritating noises with his mouth in every scene until Mark Wahlberg's tough-guy enforcer puppy, already bitter that he didn't get to keep the talking stuffed animal who had kidnapped him and his siblings, grabs his guitar from him and bashes him over the head with it, causing Sandler's character (further?) severe brain damage. Wahlberg's puppy gets sent to a canine juvenile detention center for this, but then is offered probation in exchange for promising to no longer wear oversize pants that droop below his buttocks or wear a baseball cap turned to the side of his head. As the judge enforcing these conditions reminds him: "After all, your last name *is* Wahlberg."

Morgan Freeman shines as narrator of yet another film. However, there have been reports that he was cast in this role only after Samuel L. Jackson turned it down, thus altering the film's title to *Walt Disney's 101 One-Percenters* from the original *Walt Disney's Where the F**k Are My Dalmatians?*

Another aspect of the film that may help or hurt its prospects is its graphic depictions of behavioral decadence. While some audiences might enjoy the vicarious indulgence of sex, drugs, and ripping people off, others might wonder how many Kibbles 'n Bits a dog has to snort off another dog's butt crack until enough is enough already.

Also noteworthy about this project is Scorsese's decision to move the London setting of the film's predecessor to Lower Manhattan, consistent with his and Hollywood's own history of only shooting in New York City or Los Angeles even when it is entirely unnecessary and exorbitantly expensive to do so.

With a star-studded cast so large, one would probably wonder how the sequence of actor credits would be determined. Lucky for everyone's ego in this film, this endeavor was successfully avoided: instead of being put in order of fame or celebrity, the names of the actors appear at the beginning and end of the film in a word cloud, with no one's name appearing larger than that of another. That said, there have been unconfirmed reports that George Clooney (who plays Pong, the father of the Dalmatian litter) snuck into Thelma Schoonmaker's editing bay when she was not present and saw to it that his name appeared a half-millimeter larger than all the other names, in order to assure himself that he is, after all, the top dog.

Despite the humungous cast, each one of the one hundred and one A-name stars was still paid their usual $5 to $25 million in compensation before any residuals. This will ensure that the

Disney studio will have a justifiable excuse to not pay any crew members, production assistants, or no-name actors a reasonable compensation in the months and years ahead. Disney executives and all the actor-executive producers involved in this film are said to believe their spending on the next private jet or residential compound will eventually trickle down to all the wannabe Hollywood stars and filmmakers who are right now waiting tables—or at least enough so that it will pay for the gas or the subway fare to make it to their next audition, anyway.

In a perhaps revealing grand finale, as the closing word clouds rumble in, the entire cast gets in the faces of all the aspiring actors at the Actors Studio who are overwhelmed with student loans, and flips them the bird—everyone in the cast except Alec Baldwin, that is, who almost indiscernibly mutters "cock-sucking maggots" under his breath while inexplicably moving his arms like John McCain.

Then Scorsese hurls a Golden Globe off screen, and all those top dogs go chasing after it.

NATHAN GRATZ

STUCK UNDER THE CLEETZ

Directed by Kevin Nealon. Produced by Rob Reiner.
Written by W. P. Kinsella. Starring: Zach Galifianakis,
Andy Samberg, Keanu Reeves, Jason Biggs, Dwayne
Johnson, and Ashton Kutcher.

"We know we're better than this, but we can't prove it."—Tony Gwynn

---

THE 1899 CLEVELAND SPIDERS were terrible. They lost 101 games—on the road. (Considering that current major league baseball teams play 81 games at home and 81 games on the road, this is a record that will likely never be threatened.) They played in a 9,000-seat stadium, yet drew only 6,088 fans—the entire season. Their 20-134 record remains the worst record in major league baseball history. They were so bad, in fact, that they were relegated to the minor leagues the following season. They were not, however, the 1989 New York Cleetz.

Stuck Under the Cleetz follows a painfully terrible baseball team throughout the 1989 season, from the early days of spring training, into the dog days of summer, and, finally, the pennant race and the World Series. The Cleetz finished with a 22-140 record—the second-worst record in major league baseball history—and ended the season seventy-seven games behind the World Series Champion Oakland A's, a team loaded with All-Stars and memorable players, including Billy Beane, the subject of the Oscar-nominated movie *Moneyball.*

Were it not for major league baseball's tradition of having one player from each team represented in the All-Star game every summer, the Cleetz would not have had even one All-Star on their roster; in a purely merit-based contest, none of their players would've been remotely under consideration. Thanks to those arcane MLB rules, the consensus least-deserving All-Star in history was named when Cliff Fuzzing (Galifianakis), the Cleetz' hirsute second baseman—who was batting a team-leading .184 when the midsummer classic rolled around—made the All-Star team.

The opening scene in *Stuck Under the Cleetz* reminds you of the start of pretty much any other baseball movie you've ever seen. It begins with the camera panning the outfield of a medium-size minor-league baseball stadium, on a cloudless, 82-degree day in Tucson, Arizona in March, where players are stretching, playing catch, and shagging fly balls. It's the kind of day for which people in the Midwestern and New England states pay hundreds of dollars to experience every spring when their own states are mired in a polar vortex, and everyone, player or coach, is reveling in the perfect weather. It's a good two minutes into *Stuck Under the Cleetz* before any actual words are spoken, which is fine, because Kevin Nealon's cinematography during the opening scene is nothing short of spectacular. Then the film jump-cuts across town to the Cleetz facility.

The film focuses largely on the Cleetz' "star" players: Fuzzing, left fielder Lars Larsmobile (Jason Biggs), first baseman Rigor Clovis (Andy Samberg), right fielder Dummy Hoyt (Keanu Reeves), ace pitcher Chief Bigbottom (Dwayne Johnson), and closer Kermit Gamble (Ashton Kutcher). The first dialogue begins with those six sitting in the locker room after the first day of spring training, discussing their optimism about the upcoming season. You can't help feeling optimistic along with them. Every team begins the season 0-0, after all.

The optimism fades quickly, however, after the Cleetz begin the regular season with seventeen straight losses, and soon you find yourself hoping these increasingly depressed young men just win a game. The Cleetz' manager, who is never named nor seen, but instead appears sporadically throughout the film as a shadowy figure with his voice altered, utters: "I'm telling my players to play the best that they can. And the sad thing is, most of them are."

There's a scene about fifteen minutes into *Stuck Under the Cleetz* that's been hard for me to un-see. Do you remember that part in *The Naked Gun* where they showed the baseball bloopers between innings of the Seattle Mariners-California Angels game?

Specifically, the part where a player is sliding into second base and he gets mauled by a tiger? Well, that actually happened to Fuzzing during a game. Since *The Naked Gun* was released in 1988, it wasn't a case of art imitating life—it was a case of life imitating art, or perhaps confirmation that we live in godless entropy. The scene is needlessly graphic and several minutes long—Nealon proves his mettle as an impresario of viscera, to rival H. G. Lewis— yet you can't turn away. Nor are you even the least bit confused as to how or why a fully grown, five-hundred-pound Bengal tiger got into a major league baseball stadium. You just keep watching, agape, hoping Fuzzing survives the attack.

The film slows down a bit after that, but it's just as heart-wrenching when you watch as Larsmobile gets the news he's been traded to the Minnesota Twins. For a left-handed batting glove. (There's even a short scene where callers to Minnesota sports talk radio shows complain about how the Twins got screwed in that trade.) Biggs' performance controls the screen here. When Clovis tries to console Larsmobile by telling him to keep his chin up and reminding him that it's a top-of-the-line left-handed batting glove, Larsmobile loses it. He completely snaps. Like the Fuzzing tiger attack, it's uncomfortable to watch. It's akin to when you see a bearded lady selling bananas outside of an elementary school: you want it to stop, but you can't seem to be able to do anything about it, so it just goes on.

Shortly afterward, Clovis himself gets traded. This scene itself isn't nearly as emotional as the previous one—unlike Larsmobile, Clovis was traded for an actual player—but the impetus behind it is flustering. Clovis had recently raised his batting average over .200, and the Cleetz were worried he'd be too expensive to re-sign in the offseason, so they traded him to the Los Angeles Dodgers for a minor league first baseman and cash considerations. The film follows Clovis to Los Angeles, where on his first day in town he's eating alone at the Koo Koo Roo in Santa Monica. It's pathetic in its own way.

All-Star weekend arrives, and Fuzzing, despite still being in the hospital, is named as the Cleetz' lone representative. Gamble, feeling more deserving than Fuzzing, visits Fuzzing in the hospital and punches him in the face. It's not an exaggeration to say that *Stuck Under the Cleetz* has more uncomfortable scenes than any sports film in recent memory.

As the season progresses, the film suffers from a lack of a romantic subplot, much as the Cleetz did themselves. Only one of the Cleetz players went on a date the entire season, and for legal reasons, it can't be dramatized in any medium.

Fan Appreciation Night sees Bigbottom strike out a major league record twenty-six batters in one game, a record that still stands to this day. Of course, it also sees the Cleetz lose 10-2 to the Detroit Tigers, in part because Bigbottom also walked eleven batters, hit six more, and gave up five home runs.

During the final weekend of the season, Hoyt suffered a career-ending shoulder injury. Injuries happen in sports, but usually not like this: Hoyt got injured while chasing a fly ball and running into Jarry Park's thirty-foot-high right field wall. Forty-seven times. Needless to say, it's a disturbing scene. Arguably more disturbing than the Fuzzing tiger attack.

The film ends as most feel-good baseball films end: with a World Series victory. Just not for the Cleetz.

LEO MARKS

CONSUMED

Written and directed by Shia LaBeouf. From the memoir by Saffron Mangiopel. Starring: Michael Fassbender, Elle Fanning, Fin Seekel, Laetitia Baldwin, Summit Arapetian, and Nike Doukas.

A MERE DECADE AGO, the prospect of a mainstream film with a sympathetic practicing cannibal at its center was nearly unthinkable; now, with financing from the Inclusive Consumption Society, such a film arrives, provoking only scattered protests from a faltering movement transparently laboring to console itself.

Of course, what was scandalous ten years back, when Saffron Mangiopel's memoir-cum-polemic-cum-groundbreaking-cookbook was first published, is frankly a bit ho-hum today. Resource depletion in the developed world is no longer a terrifying specter but a grinding fact of life. Our fitful, bygone yearnings for an egalitarian nation look touchingly childlike in retrospect. Very few of us today would condemn an under-resourced family's decision to shrink its consumption footprint by bi-directionalizing its food chain presence.

I'm tempted to write two reviews: one of the film as it imagines itself to be (a daring slap in the face to polite bourgeois sensibilities); the other of the film that, perhaps somewhat inadvertently, has emerged—a gentle, carefully observed story of one woman's journey from callow gastro-tourist to committed full-spectrum omnivore. But I'll try to ignore the chasm between the film as it wishes it were and the film as it is, and focus on the latter.

Director Shia LaBeouf, returning to fictional live action after finally uploading 2032's full-year-length unedited Google glass experiment *Follow Me*, sensibly excises the non-narrative components of Mangiopel's literary genre-bender (aside from an effectively mouth-watering opening-credits sautéing sequence). *Serving the Underserved: A Recovering Vegetarian's Quest to Forge Her Link in the Lateral Food Chain*, focused, naturally enough, on Mangiopel's personal transformation (even as it plainly sought to raise awareness about the bureaucratic obstacles to responsible intraspecies ingestion). LaBeouf broadens the story's scope, allotting more than half his precious minutes to the telling of the other side of the tale: the plight of the Wendigos.

Abe Wendigo, played with tautness and cunning by silver fox Michael Fassbender, is the aging patriarch of a destitute California Central Valley family, descended from successful farmers but laid low by decades of extreme weather events and dried-up aquifers. Fierce, proud, and morally complex, Wendigo schemes to bait-and-switch Mangiopel (Elle Fanning), a naïve first-time buyer obsessed with the prospect of consuming his strapping, prime-aged only son (newcomer Fin Seekel, scrumptious indeed).

Of course, perpetrators of such illegal replacement schemes face challenges greater than concocting persuasive manmeat substitutes—the real trick is permanently disappearing the putative main course. But before Wendigos *pere* and *fils* get too far in their journey down the oven-escapee underground railroad, the story takes a turn. I won't reveal whether the Wendigos carry through with their planned deceit; I'll just say that the film, much more so than the memoir, chronicles Abe Wendigo's discovery of a depth of generosity—and, one might say, tenderness—that neither he nor we imagined he possessed.

Indeed, the film's deep humanity is felt in the way it steers clear of blaming this family, or by extension the many subprime families they presumably resemble, for failing to secure adequate resourcing before choosing to reproduce. In LaBeouf's moral landscape, what matters is the journey forward, not the path one took to get here.

If the film is hard on anyone, it's the emerging global-omnivore set—our finickiness about sourcing, our occasionally self-serving concern with fair compensation for the consumed, the revival in some quarters of a (let's face it) primitive worldview that grants quasi-magical powers to metabolized heart ventricles and prefrontal cortices.

Fanning, rumored to be a convert herself, affectionately satirizes the neuroses and excesses of the contemporary urban anthro-predator.

Part of the startling appeal of the memoir was that Mangiopel didn't fit our then-current stereotype of the full-spectrum consumer—a demographic once dominated by the male, Republican, and rich. As a liberal, lesbian content producer, Mangiopel's very public decision to become an early adopter of the lateral-consumption lifestyle was a tipping point for the mainstreaming of the movement. Witnessing the stages of her conversion—her dawning recognition that the old write-a-check model of assisting the unfortunate only creates interlocking systems of dependence—is engrossing and instructive. What Abe Wendigo really wants, after all, is what we all want: a shot at dignity. One of this film's accomplishments is to confirm, subtly but clearly, that unearned access to resources, while technically life-sustaining, is rarely soul-sustaining.

We may wish for a world that lets every inhabitant procreate at their whim and die of natural causes—but it's not the world we live in. Clinging to a simplistic and time-worn humanist fantasy serves no one. Artists like Mangiopel and LaBeouf choose to abandon sentiment and explore with rigor: What are the ways we can realistically nourish each other?

Not that all is copacetic between collaborators. Mangiopel has publicly slammed LaBeouf's decision to introduce an undercurrent of erotic tension to the pivotal scene in which the anthropophage initiate goes to "meet her meat," as she waggishly phrases it. No doubt her outrage is honestly felt, but that doesn't make it justified; like many authors before her, Mangiopel may not be the most reliable interpreter of her own work. A quick kindlesearch turns up seven instances of the phrase "sinewy arms" in her single volume (three each for "meaty thighs" and "tight glutes," for what it's worth). In interviews, she openly acknowledges her objectification of young Master Wendigo but argues that it was entirely clinical and an important part of her personal growth towards fully informed consumer.

Whatever the merits of her case, onscreen it would be hard to avoid eroticism if you tried. Indeed, Fanning's Mangiopel appears to be trying—which, as with most attempts to smother passion, merely fans the flames. Seekel plays off her smoldering reticence beautifully—rejecting any hint of self-pity, his supple features register a swirl of defiance, pride, and amused recognition of the predator's inconvenient attraction to her prey.

Consumed clocks in at well under two hours. Some will question the choice to tell a complex story at such a breakneck pace. But it's enlightening to step away from today's standard thirteen-hour format, and remember how much power we used to pack into a hundred minutes of well-crafted storytelling. Admittedly, with so much to tell and so little time to tell it, the film drives forward somewhat relentlessly, only rarely repeating important plot points, and, strikingly, eliminating sponsorblasts and tweetbreaks entirely; for an old film buff, this is great nostalgic fun, but obviously will entail some attention span recalibration for the general public.

It's worth the restraint. *Consumed* ends up succeeding despite its intentions. Where it aims to be a boldly candid take on a forbidden topic, it succeeds by being knowing and wry about a settled matter. Detractors may call it ironic that Mangiopel's journey towards embracing this unfortunate family's full humanity was facilitated by her decision to eat one of its members. It's characteristic of LaBeouf's steely moral focus that he doesn't flinch from such complexity. The result is consuming indeed.

SETH BLAKE

DEATH OF A CLOWN

Directed by Wim Wenders. Written by Kilgore Trout. Cinematography by Robby Müller. Starring: Jerry Lewis, Madeline Kahn, Bruno Ganz, Peter Falk, and Willem Dafoe.

DEATH OF A CLOWN is an odd duck of a film; or, better yet, the sort of rare bird of a film that one only tends to find in moldering books devoted to the extinct—all hand-drawn, pre-Audobon baroquery in faded violet lac and cuttlefish brown blending together on the tea-colored page. A bird so odd it seems as though it could have never walked the earth (much less swum or flown it) but there it is, Latinate binomial (or in this case, its LCC number) burnished proud and chest puffed. It was "released" in 1979.

Even for those who know the story of _The Day the Clown Cried_, it is a shock to see Jerry Lewis dressed as Hitler. And though, yes, there is the sort of hamming and high-stepping and expectorating one might expect—the borschty, pidgin Hochdeutsch (Lewis, in fact, speaks little throughout the film, preferring instead to vocalize in the enthusiastic manner of Fillipo Marinetti, but when he does, he employs a rather broad take on boarding-house Yinglish); the endless _who's on first?_ heiling and re-heiling between Führer Lewis and his subordinates every time the former enters or exits a room (including _die Toilette_)—there is a tearful, torn-up pathos, too— the vaudevillian grasping at the existential—the kind that we all wanted to believe our star tried to summon in _Clown Cried_ but apparently just couldn't, at least not behind the camera (or so the stories go).

This time, it is Wim Wenders at the helm, directing from a script by Kurt Vonnegut (though he is credited, naturally, as "Kilgore Trout") and these things, it seems, made all the difference.

Contrary to what one might imagine, the light touch is not necessarily the right touch when it comes to sensitive material, and it is easy to imagine how Lewis must have gotten it wrong in his infamous first attempt at a Holocaust picture—very silly, yes, but not sublimely so; quite stupid, sure, but clearly not insane; way too much schmaltz, of course, but somehow also not enough by half— if the accounts of Harry Shearer are to be believed. Vonnegut's script—written at the fecund and dissolute height of his strange and considerable powers at a time in which, approaching fifty, marriage to highschool sweetheart Jane Cox dissolving, both he and his son Mark experienced major schizophrenic breaks— is, unlike Lewis' ill-fated attempt to find a funny, middlebrow approach to the terror at the heart of the twentieth century, just crazy enough to work.

The plot is a typically Troutian conceit enlarged, much like *Slaughterhouse Five* and *Mother Night* before it, to Wagnerian proportions by the nightmare of its real-life historical milieu rendered in striking, noirish detail by cinematographer Robby Müller. In it, Hitler is a sophisticated, joke-telling robot, sent to Earth by God (played with trademark weltschmerz by Peter Falk) as part of a routine plan to gauge the development of humanity's sense of humor and moral scruples. Confident that Hitler will be laughed out of the Munich beer hall as soon as the absurd, preprogrammed words start caroling out from his realistic mechanical mouth, heaven is instead shocked by the unironic ovation and subsequent putsch leading to the eventual deposition of the Weimar government and the robot's ascendency to the chancellorship of the so-called Third Reich.

Desperate to prevent further chaos but committed to a Leibnizian cosmological ordnung and thereby unwilling to intervene directly in human affairs, heaven sends a technician in the form of the archangel Selaphiel (an ethereal Bruno Ganz) to reprogram the beleaguered clown-bot. Despite the angel's best efforts, however, including increasing the wiggliness of the robot's signature funny-man mustache and adjusting the voice and body control knobs to their most barky and spastic settings, almost nobody seems to "get it" and Hitler's power and influence continue to go unchecked and unchallenged. The fact that Hitler himself is so obviously Jewish, and that his increasingly flagrant anti-Semitism therefore can't possibly be taken seriously, seems to escape everyone, even when Selaphiel adjusts the knob with the Magen David on it to the point where Lewis is *kvetching* in Hebrew about it being "like a sauna in here" between lines in his public speeches and mopping *schwitz* from his brow with a *tallit*. That the robot's girlfriend, Eva (Madeline Kahn playing a surreal variant of Lili von Shtupp), is herself so obviously not a goy doesn't trouble the Volk either, not as one grinning *burgher* (Ernest Borgnine in an uncredited cameo) remarks, with such "*schöne blonde haare!*"

Unable to turn the tide by the usual means, Selaphiel resorts—after a long, one-sided conversation with God via a disembodied red telephone, hanging down from heaven by a long, curly red cord somewhere over the Bavarian alps—to a final, desperate measure: fart noises. Every time Hitler gets up, sits down, bends his knees or swallows a bite of *schnitzengruben*, Selaphiel is at his elbow with an invisible whoopee-cushion in hand, or a raspberry on his lips, ready to blow. Of course, by then it is too late. Though Lewis's every reaction to the mysterious flatulence erupting constantly around him is a flash-bomb of comedic genius to an instance, captured by Wenders in a series of bathetic, balletic sequences in various palatial old-world interiors, nobody is laughing.

Having failed in his mission, the bewildered Selaphiel spends the final moments of the film disconsolately roaming Hitler's underground bunker, trying to learn about humanity by observing the play between the six young Goebbels children and their dogs. Though he sees much to redeem the race in these simple exchanges, it becomes clear to Selaphiel that humanity was simply not ready to be tested by a clown-bot as good as Hitler and that God, like all parents, had probably had a more favorable impression of his offspring than they deserved. He is relieved then when, Soviet battalions battering the door, Jodl (played with houndlike ardor by a very young Willem Dafoe) presents Hitler with a loaded luger on a velvet pillow, which Lewis—tongue out, eyes crossed, head turned like a parrot and mustache working like a very hungry caterpillar—cocks, brings slowly to his command module and finally, dispassionately, releases.

With the exception of a cuckoo bird *coo-coo*ing by and by, the credits roll in silence. And really, what else is there to say?

ERIC LAYER

QUIXOTE JONES

Directed by George Lucas. Written by Charlie Kaufman. Starring: Harrison Ford, Benicio Del Toro, Helen Mirren, and Arnold Schwarzenegger as Jürgen Von Himmelmacher.

QUIXOTE JONES, AN ADAPTATION of the formerly un-filmable *Don Quixote*, arrives in theatres today as one of the most highly anticipated films of all time—for all the wrong reasons. It's the movie equivalent of a freeway pileup: we can't help but gawk, especially after the controversy that preceded its release. From the inception, it had all the makings of a financial and artistic bomb. We were all so sure it would fail.

And we were all so wrong.

In case you've been living in a bomb shelter (which, coincidentally, is where we first meet our hero), I'll recap the film's checkered origins.

In the last century or so of filmmaking, the feat of making a *Don Quixote* film worthy of its source seemed as unlikely as Cervantes' quixotic knight slaying an actual dragon. Many tried, many failed. Orson Welles was one. He toiled over his version sporadically over several decades, as, according to Welles, "a writer works on a novel, no obligations, no time constraints. I'll finish it whenever I damn well please." Apparently he never damn well felt like it, though its specter may have haunted him to his death in 1985. Rumor has it that with his final breath, he whispered the word "Quixote" before slumping over in his chair, a glass of Chianti slipping from his lifeless fingertips.

Terry Gilliam had a better go, making it halfway through production until a dispute with Johnny Depp ground everything to a halt. Depp, perhaps still reeling from his recent channeling of Hunter S. Thompson, had decided to model his Sancho Panza after Jim Morrison. He'd show up to set in a heroin daze, swaggering in tight leather pants he refused to remove. When Gilliam threatened to fire him, Depp stormed off the set for good, saying, "You're just afraid of my freedom, man."

Besides the mediocre 1988 TV movie starring Bea Arthur as a Quixote-like housewife hopped up on pills and attacking parking meters with a mop, the masterpiece film adaptation of Cervantes' *Don Quixote* had still eluded world cinema.

When news that surrealist screenwriter Charlie Kaufman had penned an ingenious new adaptation, which not only placed Quixote in a postapocalyptic world, but also included a Kaufman-like character entering a homemade time machine to confer with Cervantes about the script, everyone pondered what brave soul would step to the helm.

Several names were tossed around: firstly, there was Spike Jonze, who had recently flopped with his remake of *The Magnificent Seven*, set in contemporary LA, and starring the surviving members of *Jackass* riding around on big wheels. Next up in the rumor mill was Peter Jackson, but when *The Scrolls of Destiny*, his six-part adaptation of a Dungeons & Dragons campaign he'd led in high school, left both critics and audiences stupefied, he retreated into the New Zealand mist. Even Spielberg had shown interest, but opted instead for *Auschwitz! Auschwitz!*, the upcoming third part of his World War II trilogy, and yes, unfortunately, it's a musical. When at last the trade papers revealed the chosen one, a nation's collective jaw dropped: George Lucas? Seriously???

Jaws fell further when a cast sheet was leaked to the press. Benicio del Toro as Sancho Panza seemed sensible enough, but who would play the iconic titular knight, the delusional old man that nevertheless captures the hearts and minds of young and old?

Harrison *fucking* Ford?!?!

Yes, Harrison FUCKING Ford, who gives the performance of a lifetime. And George Lucas, who obliterates his marred reputation following the god-awful *Star Wars* prequels to deliver a film that's far from "kid-friendly." One can only think he took to heart the gang of Star Wars geeks who made headlines last year when they broke into Lucas's ranch dressed as Stormtroopers and held him hostage, their only demands a written admittance of the suckiness of the prequels and a promise never to direct another *Star Wars*. (*Ed. note: The kidnappers are still at large at present time.*)

"Is this another *Indiana Jones* sequel?" is the question everyone's been asking.

Answer: only in the most delightfully screwed-up way possible. It's more of a deconstruction of a Joseph Campbell myth: the hero's journey, which, not coincidentally, also served as a blueprint for the original *Star Wars*. In Kaufman and Lucas's version, instead of the protagonist reluctantly thrust into the role of savior, undergoing a spiritual transformation, and ultimately triumphing against evil, in this *Quixote*, Ford, known only as "Jones," ordains himself a hero, naively embracing the cliché without any seeming cause. All of his attempts to "save the world" end in tragic humiliation, and we laugh along with all the supporting players at his buffoonery, even if, like the original Quixote, it only makes him more tragically human.

Similarly, Lucas and Ford did very little right with their careers this century and had not only been written off, but were at times verbally abused by even their most ardent fans. (Who can forget the man who flew over Lucas Ranch, skywriting the words "Suck it, George"?) These were two men with something to prove, if they cared to. Many rumors circulated about their preparation: there were those blurry cellphone videos of the two of them drunk and naked in a fountain at the Bellagio, reports of motorcycle trips into Mexico, a shamanic sweat-lodge initiation on Harrison's Wyoming ranch, and an apparent trek into the Mojave desert, where they subsided for several days on only mescaline tea and Vitamin Water.

Whether true or not, it's clear from the film that they at least found their muses.

Perhaps the hallucinogens wiped their minds clean of past atrocities and allowed them to connect with the unhinged imagination of Kaufman. In his script, Cervantes' novel serves as a jumping-off point to explore not only an America after a total ruin but the very soul of a man who was once its biggest star.

The film opens on the enigmatic Jones, locked in his aforementioned bomb shelter. He bides time, eating beans from a can and making origami animals, including a paper-maché unicorn, a nod to *Blade Runner,* the first of many references to the participant's previous films. He confers with an imaginary friend, a clump of his own hair which he's nicknamed "Chewy." After dinner, he combs through a small library of DVDs. He considers a few titles: *Citizen Kane, Brazil,* (an acknowledgment of the directors who failed to film *Quixote,* perhaps?) until he finally settles on one. Yes, it's *Raiders of the Lost Ark.*

This could have been gimmicky (or worse, self-promotional), but it works on two levels. This Jones could actually be Ford, reliving his glory days. Or it could be just an ordinary old man suffering dementia and placing himself in all the movies he watches. Ford's craggy, deeply lined face observes his young self as he performs heroic feats, and something stirs in him. He transforms before our eyes, adopting the steely reserve of a hero again. Delusional though he may be, we can't help but half-root for him to return to his former, glorious self.

Instead, he makes a fool of himself. After dressing himself in armor made of tinfoil, he makes a vow to himself in a mirror, "To rid the planet of all evil." Outside, the unnamed town is in shambles, with survivors living in essentially seventeenth-century conditions and violence ruling the day. The world gone mad, Jones' madness is barely noticed at first. No one takes him seriously until he meets Sancho Panza (Benicio del Toro), a former drug addict turned half-mad, half-savage conspiracy gun-nut (if he's modeled after any rock star, it might be Ted Nugent). They squabble at first, but gradually Sancho softens to Jones' fervent hope and naive belief in the triumph of good and joins him in search of evil to rid the world of.

A good chunk of the film follows terrain similar to the book, updated to modern times. Instead of commandeering a tired old horse as his steed, Jones rides a rusty mountain bike, while Sancho rides, naturally, a temperamental Segway. Instead of windmills, Jones fights oil pumps—an obvious environmental metaphor, perhaps, but hilarious to watch.

And that's really the genius of this film: for all its dark undertones, it remains lighthearted, deft, and perceptive of humanity's foils. Lucas's previous powers are at last fully revived: the vivid imagination from the first three *Star Wars*, the hopeful humanism of *American Graffiti*, and the dystopic vision of *THX1138*—all are present in this film, with a dose of the existential to boot.

Part of the joy of this film is the nuanced performances he gets out of the many cameos. There's something inspired about casting Helen Mirren as the love interest that inspires all of Jones' exploits, not only because it harkens back to the Ford/Mirren matchup of *Mosquito Coast* but also that it's nice to see old man Ford actually going for someone from his own generation, for once.

The film gains extra weight (pun intended) with the arrival of George (a chubby Arnold Schwarzenegger, who appears to have finally given up his workout routine, or at least his steroid diet). The fact that this is his finest film since *The Terminator* perhaps goes without saying, but the real revelation here is that, for the first time, he's *acting*, not as some juiced-up version of himself but as an actual *character*. At the risk of becoming too meta (which Kaufman never seems to shy away from), Arnold plays a pretentious, Fassbender-like Austrian filmmaker who harnesses his last chance at success by filming Jones and Sancho's exploits. He's constantly staging conflicts and reenacting events they've only just enacted, calling into question the very idea of "filmmaking" in a world gone mad (and not so far away from our own).

This *had* to be a Lucas/Ford film, and the reasons become more and more apparent as the film dissects the creative process, and the hazards of success. Ford is constantly hounded for autographs by starving cannibals who, a minute later, want to rip his limbs off. Perhaps the only sequence that comes off gratuitous is a *Deliverance*-like fever dream sequence, in which Ford hallucinates getting gang-raped by several Jar Jar Binks–like creatures, one even taunting, "Me'sa wanna hear old man squeal like pig." It's the one case of Lucas pushing the *meta* one step too far, but, luckily, a short one.

When *Quixote Jones* was chosen to close Cannes earlier this year, critics (this one included) scoffed. This was the final nail in the coffin of a once-great festival now succumbing to the almighty dollar. When a frail, rail-thin Lucas took the stage, the audience let out a collective gasp. He informed us they had just delivered the final print that very morning. "I hope you enjoy my little film. It's very near and dear to my heart."

Something in his earnest delivery told me we might be in for something unexpected. When the credits rolled and the entire audience rose to its feet in applause, there was only one person left sitting: Lucas himself. A photographer caught the moment: he looked…dissatisfied. When the Palme d'Or was later announced, going, naturally, to Lucas, he took to the stage calmly amidst the thunderous applause.

"This…" he began, and we all expected him to follow with "… *is the greatest honor of my life*." Instead, defying expectations yet again, Lucas went on, "…is bullshit. Total fucking BULLSHIT!" Smashing his award on the stage floor and hurrying offstage amid a flurry of gasps and flashbulbs, critics claim it was his attempt to manufacture a "von Trier moment," cementing a new reputation as a "troubled auteur." Whether planned or not, no one could doubt his conviction. He hasn't spoken to the press since, and no one knows exactly where he is. Could he be hiding away in a bomb shelter himself, tinkering, editing and reediting his magnum opus in a futile attempt to finally get it right?

Time will tell. For now, we have *Quixote Jones*, a thrilling, thought-provoking, and wild mess of a masterpiece, and a fine way to spend two hours while awaiting the inevitable end of all things.

DAVID W. HARRINGTON

NOAH MEANS YES

Directed by Rob Reiner and Roman Polanski. Starring: Katherine Heigl, Joseph Gordon-Levitt, Russell Brand, Jonah Hill, Seann William Scott, Paul Rudd, Vince Vaughn, Ving Rhames, Amanda Seyfried, and Amanda Bynes.

NOAH MEANS YES, CODIRECTED by veterans Rob Reiner and Roman Polanski, is the film equivalent of a cuddly baby chimp that you adopt from the wild who then eats your face off. At least forty-five minutes of the film will please the women who want nothing more than to see Joseph Gordon-Levitt work his alchemy of turning unrequited love into true romance.

The final scenes of *Noah* might please some of the unlucky boyfriends who are dragged along to sit through a supposed chick flick. They'll also please the serial killers, critics of rom-com fantasy, and those of us who are bored with the genre and never thought we'd be surprised by a major studio again. (Whether this film will actually get distribution is another matter.)

I'll go out on a limb here and say *Noah Means Yes* succeeds where *500 Days of Summer* and *He's Just Not That Into You* fail. At first it appears to follow the traditional rom-com arc before it veers off wildly into territory more reminiscent of *The Shining*. As such, the movie is less a romantic comedy than a commentary on the creepiness of the genre itself: in movieland, the path to a woman's heart is often blind persistence, whereas in the real world, persistence in the pursuit of a woman's heart might involve chipping away at her sternum.

The movie's confusing but ultimately genius bipolarity is a result of its curious production history. About half was filmed in New York, but Rob Reiner threw his back out while choking at Katz's Delicatessen three weeks into the shoot and was unable to travel to Temptation Resort in Mexico to film the crucial second half of the picture.

"We needed a Jewish director, and we needed someone with the balls to do romance right," says an executive at MGM who asked not to be identified. "Roman wanted to get back to North America, and we knew he'd be perfect. He loved the film, loved the idea of Temptation Resort, and knew this was a chance to come back on his own terms. The only thing he asked for was a little creative control over the script."

The film begins with Noah Asher (Gordon-Levitt), an entry-level financial professional who lives and works in Manhattan with his best buds Adam (Jonah Hill) and Hannibal (Seann William Scott), whom he also went to college with. When not working, The Bros, as they're called, try to help Noah overcome a recent heartbreak (she cheated on him and then left) by wing-manning him through meaningless hookups with a string of women, most of which end with Noah crying alone in the bathroom until his friends lure him out with consoling romantic comedies and popcorn.

It's clear that these romantic comedies, which Noah confesses to having watched all his life, serve as training films for Noah and The Bros; even when not openly discussed or watched by the characters, you see rom-com DVD covers, movie posters, in-flight entertainment options, and background shots of them playing in bars and at house parties.

The usual happens when Noah and The Bros' firm, headed by Paul Rudd and Vince Vaughn, brings in Angelina (Katherine Heigl), a quirky Midwesterner (read: Annie Hall dumbed down and at the mall) who is oblivious to all the attention she generates.

Noah, of course, falls madly in love, inspiring the requisite scenes of him stumbling over himself to win her affection even as she falls down the stairs on her first day at work and farts at a board meeting.

After a string of solid "nos" from Angelina, the diligent Noah finally secures a lunch date during which she tells him of her childhood in Kansas and her dreams of making it big in something one day. "I won't be a secretary forever," she sighs. "I just want the normal life, a good career, a devoted man, and a few kids."

From the scenes we've seen of Angelina at home causing explosions in the microwave, melting blouses under the iron, and flipping through iPhoto albums of bungled jobs, internships, and relationships, we know her destiny will be bleak—though most of us expect spinster rather than spinning on a spit like a pig.

When Noah reaches his hand across the table for hers and confesses he wants this life for himself and that he wants her, it's clear the kiss he intends to plant next will land somewhere in the Pad Thai. At this point, and throughout the Reiner portion of the movie, the tone is striking: Noah's repeated advances are treated as heroic, and we get the sense he will be rewarded for them as soon as Angelina realizes his devotion to her makes him the one.

Just as Angelina scrunches her nose and pulls away, saying she reluctantly agreed to this "friendly" lunch, her girlfriends happen to stop in. Angelina embarrasses herself and the Amandas (played by real life Amandas Seyfried and Bynes) by lighting her cloth napkins on fire and spilling water all over the table.

When she runs off to the bathroom in tears, her friends tell Noah that Angelina will always be alone because she's just so weird. They find her disgusting. She's a virgin. She can't keep a job. She's driven away dozens of boyfriends. "Wait, you don't actually like her, do you, Noah? Dude, just celebrate the fact that you dodged a bullet when she blew up your lunch."

Hijinks ensue as the Amandas and The Bros try in vain to take Noah from the chase. Angelina sets very clear "just friends" boundaries, and given the amount of time they spend together, you doubt either has time for another pal: They eat lunch together daily, take shopping trips, go to museums and tourist spots, and hike through city parks. Meanwhile, the four sidekicks find themselves increasingly drawn together, hooking up in a bewildering array of configurations like the side plots in a Shakespearian love comedy.

One drunken night, The Bros show the Amandas secret video footage taken of Noah sleeping with a string of rebound women. The Amandas show the videos to Angelina, who is horrified. Although quirky and pretty, Angelina turns out to be a prude who thinks intimacy should be reserved for married couples—and then only once or twice a year on special holidays. "Not even oral?" one Amanda asks. "What about in the butt?"

Angelina dumps Noah as a friend when they next meet, which also happens to be the date at Coney Island at which he'd planned to confess his love and plant a real kiss. Alone in line for the Cyclone, rose in his hand, it's hard to see a way out for Noah now.

Even though we're only halfway through the movie by this point, it seems like everything should be over. And it pretty much is, until Paul Rudd and Vince Vaughn announce they're taking everyone on an all-expenses-paid company retreat to Temptation Resort on the Yucatan Peninsula, where they can work on company bonding.

Temptation Resort is pure *Sarah Marshall* territory, down to the group's guide, the charming Mickey (Russell Brand), who leads them in trust building and motivational exercises while taking a particular interest in Angelina, thus setting up Mickey and Noah as mismatched rivals. It all goes to hell when, noticing Angelina return Mickey's affections, Noah punches him in the face. The men hold Noah back, he watches Angelina lead Mickey away, and the next morning the two walk in together holding hands, Mickey with a black eye and Angelina in her clothing from the night before. Polanski has entered the building.

I won't ruin the final few minutes of the movie, but even though Polanski stays true to Reiner's Randy Newman score and rosy camera filters, things get gritty and dark. Noah books a flight to New York the next morning, vowing to change everything in his life. "Fuck this hotel: It's nothing but a dry hump, tempting me to give up. And fuck love too. Fuck everything I've believed. I'm tired of the same old shtick. The only way to get a woman is to *get* her." From this point forward, it's worth noting that the movie references switch from rom-com classics to fare by Kubrick and Hitchcock, even theater like *Woyzeck* and Artaud.

That night, Noah gets deathly drunk, and when The Bros and his concerned bosses find him by the water, he's talking to Tevin (Ving Rhames) about his problems. Tevin, whose new bride has just left him on their honeymoon, goes on about how you have to be firm with a woman and show her who's boss. "They don't know who they are or what they want without us. In fact, whenever they say or do no to me, I know that's when I got to show them yes."

It turns out that Paul Rudd and Vince Vaughn have also been recently spurned, and that The Bros have been abandoned by the Amandas. Led by Tevin, the men swear a blood oath that night, stripping to their underwear, carving the word *Yes* into each other's chests with seashells, and baptizing themselves in the bloody surf while sharks circle offshore.

As the movie brings us to the primal scene, I had flashbacks to *Heart of Darkness* and *Apocalypse Now*. And in fact, in the final moments, Polanski explicitly paints Mickey as an inverted Kurtz and echoes the slaughter of Brando/the ox. Armed with tiki torches and broken bottles from the resort's open bar, the men crash a staff/guest swinger's party in Mickey's suite, drag the new couple out by the hair, and haul them to the top of a faux Mayan temple where life and death will mingle midway between heaven and the underworld.

ADAM KAPLAN

BACK TO THE FUTURE V

Directed and produced by Robert Zemeckis. Starring: Christopher Lloyd, Floyd Mayweather Jr., Bobby Dean, Julianne Hough, Dennis Miller, and Michael Clarke Duncan.

Reviewed by Kenneth E. Topper

Get it down!
Get it, Brown!
Cram it in there, Mister Brown!

THIS LITTLE DITTY IS rasped by a circle of slaves as John Brown, abolitionist, assists Dr. Emmet Brown, scientist and cousin from the future, as John attempts to insert a thermogenic bomb in an African American freedom fighter's colon. Emmet, in one of his frequent action hero quips, mentions that there will be no bodies to lie "a moldin' in the grave," after Mister Cobble (the escaped slave whose insides house the weapon) detonates "the fucker" outside of the courthouse in Harper's Ferry, Virginia. Mister Cobble (the aforementioned character, not the six-foot, 332-pound red-shirt sophomore defensive tackle on the Kentucky Institute of Technology's football team, who, upon learning of the existence of such a character in such a film, declared that he totally wished he had a Delorean) then gives an Oscar-worthy speech about freedom, the human spirit, and his eviscerated mother's potato farm in Torrington, Connecticut.

This scene raises several important questions. Does Robert Zemeckis have early onset Alzheimer's? Do we live in such a moral vacuum that a montage depicting Harriet Tubman and Fredrick Douglass being reconstructed as slavery-fighting cyborgs can be played for laughs? Is it possible this film was created for the express purpose of giving me, Kenneth E. Topper, film reviewer and crusader for artistic integrity, a fucking brain aneurysm?

Here is what happened to me after I left the theater. My date, who, by the way, is actually named Emily Post, demands to be taken to a retro ice cream parlor. She is either disgusted or confused by the film, it is hard to tell which, yet is clearly afraid to speak because she is at least vaguely aware that I am a film reviewer. I found her on a Christian dating site I frequent even though I am not a Christian exactly. I use that site because I find the girls there tend to ask fewer questions and are impressed by vagaries. I choose to see *BTTF 5* because I figured it would be innocuous. I didn't think at the time that some Christians might consider time travel a form of evil magic. Also, I didn't want a repeat of the *Training Day* incident. I took a larger yet still pretty-in-the-face girl to see the Fuqua and made the mistake of mentioning the time I smoked crank out of a coke can in Redondo Beach with some youths that worked at the T-shirt shop and the large girl, who moved quite well for a large girl, exclaimed she needed to buy deli meats for lunch the next day and took off her heels and ran.

I was drinking more then and I might have followed her for a while and yelled some. Anyway, since then I have developed a system for movie dates. No films with rape unless the rape is avenged by gun violence, no movies about the removal or discovery of a rogue penis, no films with bespectacled Jews. I tend to favor remakes of films or sequels of films that might have been beloved in the date's childhood, and anything with blacks and whites working together to solve crimes.

Here is what she ordered at the parlor: orange sorbet. It makes no sense, I know, but at that point I did not level accusations because I thought that there was still a chance I could make her see the worm. I have made exactly nine girls see the worm in the last sixteen months. I met four of them on the Christian dating site. Two had children so I am not sure they count.

I ordered a milkshake because when at an ice cream parlor, I sure as shit order product with some fucking lactose. She went on about her sorority, which served Christ and hot meals every other Sunday. I thought for a moment about her ankle socks. I thought about my cat and the plastic pee protector on my bed. I imagined time travel and attempted to conceive of a time in my life I would like to revisit.

If I were Jesus, this is how I would play it: I would return to Earth in a darkened theater and take a seat next to a girl in a skirt. I would use my magic to mesmerize her and then I would take her behind the handicap seats and worm it in. I would do it during the good stuff, the big releases. I would let one thirteen-year-old watch so he could have a role model. Then I would turn into a bat and disappear.

NEAL POLLACK

DR. STRANGE

Directed by Joss Whedon. Starring: Ryan Gosling, Miranda Cosgrove, Josh Brolin, Aziz Ansari, Ken Jeong, and Samuel L. Jackson.

REVIEWING A PRODUCT LIKE *Dr. Strange*, the latest superhero tentpole from Marvel Pictures, is like telling people whether or not they should eat at Subway on a road trip. The promotion for this picture has been so all-encompassing, for so long, that opinion-forming seems pointless. Everyone who already cares about continuity errors has already seen the previews at Comi-Con or online, and everyone else is going to get sucked indoors by the promise of air-conditioning and a forty-eight-ounce soda, caught in the whirl of cosmic marketing forces one-hundred times more powerful than the cone-like extradimensional portals that the movie's protagonist is so fond of summoning.

A short *précis* is due to those of you who've been undertaking useful work in the South Pacific or Africa the last few months and have therefore missed the relentless bus billboards: Stephen Strange, played by Ryan Gosling, is a thinly handsome eccentric who lives in a block-long mansion in Greenwich Village. Because of the price of the real estate in that neighborhood, we must assume, this house has been in his family a long time. Dr. Strange also happens to be a master of the occult, as well as the world's greatest magician.

By that, we don't mean that he pulls rabbits out of his hat, though; in the movie's lightest and most human-scaled scene, he wows the kids at his niece's birthday party with tricks that would make even Penn Jillette shut up and take notice. Instead, Dr. Strange practices the kind of magic that involves summoning spirits and channeling the energy fields of magical cubes and generally trying to find hidden objects of the type that serve as plot devices for many badly-written comic books. He puts on lavish robes and utters ridiculous incantations in what appears to be a pidgin Balkan dialect. There's a monster and a rival and a pretty girl and a few guest stars from the Marvel Universe to keep matters interesting, and it all degenerates into a globular mess of noise and CGI ghost hysterics by the end.

The Twitterverse initially raged at the choice of Gosling to play a minor comic book character of whom most people have never heard, but his casting turns out to be the only thing that keeps this thing from being sucked into an abyss created by the demon Dormammu. Like Johnny Depp, but without the affectations or prancing, Gosling has the ability to make listless intellectualism seem heroic. Strange gets blasted a few times by cosmic rays, and he certainly dishes out the magical punishment in large doses, but he doesn't land a single punch and never lifts anything heavier than a crystal ball. When he's not battling extra-worldly demons, he lounges on the couch, checking his iPhone. He's soft, wimpy, and vaguely condescending to those who don't share his vast learning, like a Pitchfork reviewer in a velvet cloak.

The film's villain, a rival magician and East Village occult bookstore owner, is played by a miscast Josh Brolin, who's woefully upstaged by the series of bulbous appendages that begin to sprout from his body after he summons a Lovecraftian demon from the depths of hell. Miranda Cosgrove, TV's beloved *iCarly*, makes her adult-movie debut as Strange's assistant and purported love interest, and all she does is bubble and squeak; though as a Nickelodeon product she knows how to gamely react while getting slimed. The relationship between Gosling and Cosgrove is the worst of *Dr. Strange's* many flaws. He comes on like a creepy uncle at summer vacation, and she seems blissfully unaware of his perverted intentions. Meanwhile, Aziz Ansari and Ken Jeong shuck-and-jive their way around as a couple of street hustlers, refugees from another movie. It's hard to believe they don't shout

"Mammy!" when—spoiler alert!—the Fantastic Four rush in toward movie's end to save the day.

This being a Marvel joint, Samuel Jackson shows up to tie it all together, giving us all the feeling that we've just watched a two-hour superhero cartoon block on Disney XD. But therein lies the problem when every must-see movie involves a superhero, each less well-known to the general public than the next. Dr. Strange may be the world's greatest sorcerer, but the magic that we all felt when, say, the first Batman or Spider-Man movies appeared has long since dissipated. Other than, say, the impossible copyright-prevented dream of a *Hulk vs. Superman* movie, there's nothing left to wow and surprise us. *Dr. Strange* is the Keyser Söze of comic book movies. A little flash, a little dash, and then, after a week or two and $125 million, poof! He's gone.

SCOTT DOMINIC CARPENTER

SAVING ELECTRA

*Directed by Phil Traill. Starring: Jack Black, Megan Fox,
Sylvester Stallone, Tobey Maguire. With Judy Greer and
Shaquille O'Neal.*

CASTING JACK BLACK AS a romantic lead is a bold move. After his 2005 appearance in the cable series *Laser Farts*, some assumed the Whoopee Cushion of his career had gasped its last. But in 2006 came *Nacho Libre* (another nod in the direction of flatulence?) and soon thereafter *Be Kind Rewind* (2008). Not classics, I admit, but with one furry hand after another, Black clawed his way out of the pit and began to scale the heights—rather like the great ape King Kong (with whom he shares so many features, minus the size). And as *Kung Fu Panda* went franchise, he could legitimately pummel his man-boobs and roar. Women everywhere should be taking notice.

This backstory of triumph—or rather, of victorious return after defeat—is what drew me to *Saving Electra*. And with Black playing the lead role of Bruce Meek, there was no way this film could succumb to the cookie cutter of romantic comedy.

Or should I say, romantic *drama*? There's a wistfulness about Black we never detected in the swashbuckling of the Nacho or behind the jiggling belly of Po. But think about it. Do you really have to look like Robert Pattinson to know the bite of lost love or the sting of ridicule? Hardly! Why are thickset men—especially if they're compact and hirsute (which scientists call a sign of vigor)—so often deemed unfit for romantic duty? It's been that way since Quasimodo and Esmeralda, or even Snow White with her faithful (but only platonically loved) companions. Women refuse to acknowledge it, but shorter, stockier, hairier men have feelings, too. They've suffered. They've taken it on their double chin. Trust me.

That boxing metaphor comes thanks to Sylvester Stallone, who plays Bubba, Bruce Meek's dad in *Saving Electra*. Those of you who remember Stallone—himself rather short and hairy, and now thickening a bit in the middle—as a stone-faced, droopy-eyed Rambo (or Rocky Balboa or Judge Dredd or Jack Carter or Frankie Delano) will be moved by his performance here, especially the scene where he counsels young Bruce and manages to raise his right eyebrow. The culmination of a fine career.

This is the kind of film you'll enjoy with a cold beer in your fist. Of course, you don't get longnecks at the multiplex, which is why I prefer watching movies at home. Yes, the restraining order has something to do with it, too, but now the living room is practically a home theater. Just scoot the dishes and overdue bills to the side and put your feet on the coffee table. You have total freedom that way. No worrying about other people. Or putting on trousers. (I don't care how short they are; hairy legs need to breathe.) And besides, it's good to be here in case the phone rings. Which it could. You never know.

Bruce Meek is a beer drinker, too. That's right: he's not prancing about, holding his little pinkie out from a champagne flute. Nobody does that in this movie except for Trent (flat-bellied Tobey Maguire—as if Peter Parker could ever be a turn-on!), who swoops in to steal away Electra Miles (Megan Fox) from Bruce. It's a story as old as time: a brooding, soon-to-be-successful and charmingly scruffy beau loses his jaw-droppingly gorgeous, newly anointed poet girlfriend to a guy with a size-fifteen neck (and hardly a hair on it; seriously, has Maguire even gone through puberty yet?), and who happens to be a psychiatrist specializing in issues of low self-esteem. Not that *he* has any such problems. Why should he? Especially since he practically abducts Bruce's girlfriend, using his psycho-mumbo-hocus-jumbo-pocus. And although Bruce struggles mightily to recover her, that is, to "save" her, as the title implies, she—spoiler alert—ultimately remains with "Trent" (is that even his real name?), whose "good looks" are less chiseled than putty-knifed.

Saving Electra is stirring. I had to take breaks to hold myself together. Which gave me time to make nachos and grab another beer. I checked for phone messages. Once or twice I peeked through the telescope, just to see what was going on across the street. (She wasn't home yet.) Then back to work on the sofa!

I don't mean to set this up as the greatest movie of all time. Maybe just the decade. What holds it back, frankly, is the pacing. Length isn't the problem. (It's a one-six-pack-er.) Nor do I think every story has to have a happy ending. Although, would it have killed Phil Traill to make good on the title and let Electra be "saved"? But there's just no time for that. In fact, the first sixty minutes are spent on backstory, a year in the life of Bruce and Electra, as the protagonist broods in his existential funk, struggling to help his girlfriend see *at every single turn* why her short-term success as a "poet" (and a minimalist one at that!) is responsible for his inability to put a brush to the canvas, or compose a single measure at the piano, or apply for that fast-food job—whichever one he decides to do!

We've all been there, right? One thing's for sure: Traill knows how to portray loss, keeping the camera tight and close on Bruce's grimaces, and even on Bubba's stoic scowl (just before the eyebrow twitch). There's a stunning shot of Black after he receives Electra's goodbye note. (She sends it from her iPad, and just by iMessage, not even the guts for FaceTime!) As the camera draws back, the living room grows around him, swallowing him up like a paunchier, hairier, and smaller Jonah in the belly of the whale.

But he scrabbles his way out. After all, he's supposed to save her, right? Soon he's swinging by her house, "crossing paths" at the grocery store, and even popping up at all her dates—or, as Trent calls them, "sessions." ("How does he keep finding you?" Trent asks. Hah! Remember Electra's iPad? Thank God for GPS. It's the greatest. Am I right, or what?) Anyway, Bruce calls her some names and bellows outside her window in the middle of the night. The police get involved. This kind of romantic diligence used to be rewarded. (Think Benjamin Braddock courting Elaine Robinson in *The Graduate*.)

They can call it stalking if they want, but the intentions are good.

As Electra slips through Bruce's stubby fingers, there's this throbbing background music. What *is* that? I thought. Some kind of drum? Or a bagpipe? The joke was on me: it was me, blubbering. Who did I feel more sorry for? Bruce, destined to be a lone-wolf hero? Or Electra, condemned to a life of bourgeois numbness, the horror of which she remained blind to? No doubt about it: her loss outstripped his by a mile.

The drama is heightened by a catchy cameo by Shaquille O'Neal (yes, very tall, but developing a bit of a belly—he's just human, after all) and a powerful role by Judy Greer (Amy), who tries to mediate between her two best friends and who, if you replay sections of the DVD over and over, clearly shows a bit of a thing for Bruce that she's too shy to express.

Some movies just resonate with their age; they pulse with a generation. No sooner had I finished than I pressed play again, and right after the second viewing I drained my last Bud (Lite, so the gut's not from that) and got on the Internet to order a copy for a certain special someone I know, whose name starts with "M," who lives really close by, who probably still reads my column, and who I think will find *Saving Electra* pretty damn relevant. Yes indeedy. Pretty goddamn relevant.

Everyone should see this movie. God knows why it's only on DVD. But order it. Express shipping. Then sit your fat hairy ass down and click play. Have a beer. It's not too late. Get busy *Saving Miranda*.

SARAH LABRIE

SIX CATS WHO LOOK LIKE JESUS

Directed by Lars von Trier. Starring: six cats who look like Jesus, Jennifer Lawrence, and Tyler Perry.

IT'S NOT AS IF we weren't warned. When it premiered last spring at the SXSW Film Festival, critics touted *Six Cats Who Look Like Jesus* as the film that would finally change moviegoing—and indeed our experience as humans on this planet—for good.

"We got it all wrong before," wrote an in-retrospect fairly desperate-sounding Manohla Darghis for the *New York Times*. "We were wrong about everything. But…how could we have known?"

The problem with writing a review of *Six Cats Who Look Like Jesus* is that there's no precedent for it. There's actually never been a movie like this before—in fact, I'm not even sure if you can call it a movie. Does forty-five minutes of GIFs repurposed from nineties sitcoms, 2000s romantic comedies, and the Beyoncé Superbowl half-time show count as a plot? Does it even matter?

The other major difficulty with trying to review *Six Cats Who Look Like Jesus* is that you, as a human being on the Internet, already know everything there is to know about it. Its YouTube channel alone has seven billion fans, making it statistically impossible for you not to be one of them. And, even if you're somehow not one, you've read the most recent angry think piece about it published on the *Awl* which, as of this writing, has been shared by over ten million readers. Which is to say that, with every tweet, click and post, we allowed this project to come into being. We did this. All of us. *Six Cats Who Look Like Jesus* is all of our faults.

Brought to you by the team of venture capitalists responsible for Groupon, *Six Cats Who Look Like Jesus* stars a selection of six cats, one of whom does actually look quite a lot like Jesus. Aside from that, it consists primarily of Vines starring a Sausalito teen who looks like Justin Bieber running his fingers through his hair. Viewers are encouraged to like and comment on each six-second vignette in real time.* The film also breaks every two minutes so viewers can tweet, text, and post movie theater selfies. A social media intern known only as @MCKENNA1996 crowdsources a new ending at each screening, so that, depending on the number of retweets, likes, favorites, and @replies, *Six Cats Who Look Like Jesus* culminates with either A) a wedding between two attractive white people, B) a Macklemore concert, or C) a livestream of Jennifer Lawrence on her laptop at a Beverly Hills Coffee Bean cycling between checking her Gmail, updating Facebook, and sub-tweeting Emma Stone.

Though the cast features dozens of teenagers famous on Instagram for no discernible reason, the real star of this movie is you. In fact, there are no credits. *Six Cats Who Look Like Jesus* ends when a tiny pinpoint of green light switches on at the very top of the screen. The camera turns on the audience, reflecting back to it a picture of itself, steady and unwavering. The light remains on, presumably recording even as the audience gets up and leaves. It may still be recording. I haven't been able to turn my cell phone camera off since the screening, and neither has anyone I know.

With a first weekend haul of over $9 billion, *Six Cats Who Look Like Jesus* is the highest-grossing film of all time. Meanwhile, the soundtrack has sold more than every other CD put out this year combined. Featuring new singles by Taylor Swift, Rita Ora, Katy Perry, Rihanna, Nicki Minaj, and Iggy Azalea, each song appears to have been specially engineered to distract from the fact that, due to the spontaneous complete melting of the ice caps, we're all being forced to forage for food—

Listen.

We could fight this, you know.

We could ride out to the desert where the screens are blank as closed eyes and the text alerts can't reach us. Where the tumblers are full of bourbon and the only things tweeting are the sparrows in the clean morning air. We could start over in a place where you don't know what your seventh-grade lab partner's minutes-old infant looks like and I don't know what my grandmother's Facebook personality turned out to be.

I'd follow you there.

I'd like that.

A sequel to *Six Cats Who Look Like Jesus*, tentatively titled *Puppies Falling Asleep on Babies*, is already in the works and scheduled to be released for free online, in theaters, on your tablets and iPhones, on television, and into your dreams via drone every day for the rest of your life or until the universe implodes in a fiery heat death, whichever comes first.

*Delivered via innovative technology that turns every monitor into a touch screen, Six Cats Who Look Like Jesus *features real-time updates from viewers across the world who can log in and, after watching a brief ad—well here, why don't you watch that brief ad first, and then we'll tell you?* **

**The above is an actual paragraph excerpted from the film's electronic press release. It's important to note that I did not click the link because I was afraid to. A colleague of mine did but wasn't much help, as, immediately after doing so, she resigned from her position as a journalist at this esteemed publication and took her children to "live" with her mom in Fresno for a while…as if that would help anything. But still. You can never be sure. [nervous laugh]. Oh, God. It's too late already, isn't it? It was always already too late.

TOM DIBBLEE

BABY ON FIRE

*Directed by Neil Labute. Produced by Scott Rudin.
Cinematography by John Seale, ASC, ACS. Music by
Michael Penn. Starring: Aaron Eckhart, Kate Hudson,
and Bud Cort.*

BABY ON FIRE IS a movie about a number of things: birth, flames, life, death, scarring, surgery, hospitals, maternity, paternity, and the unexpected consequences of sexual intercourse. It is not, however, about many other things: toddlerhood, adolescence, the teenage years, basic healthy life-development paths, growing up, responsible parenting, friendship, redemption, religious fervor, or feats of heroism. It makes use of a style marked by a number of influences: most notably, Christopher Guest and Baz Luhrmann. And yet it opens the doors on new terrain for filmmakers: most notably the very, very hot uterus of a woman named Gwen Mackey.

Gwen has a problem, but she doesn't know what it is. She knows she's pregnant, but she can't imagine why the baby inside her stomach emits such an insanely high level of heat. In the film's opening scene, she holds her hand over her bulge and remarks to her husband, Jed, "Feel here. The baby is kicking and it's incredibly hot." Jed puts his hand on his wife's stomach. His hand, as promised, becomes incredibly hot. He pulls it away, and—devoted to his wife but, one begins to suspect, marked by a uselessness that might have repercussions once a fireball shoots out from between his wife's legs and across the room—goes to the kitchen and fills a freezer bag with ice.

He puts the freezer bag on Gwen's stomach, the ice melts instantly, everything goes to hell, and the baby's not even born yet.

Have you ever noticed that there are a lot of movies and books in the world that are basically regular domestic dramas except there's something really weird going on in the family that acts sort of like a supermassive metaphor but also like a plot hook so big that it relieves the author or filmmaker of the responsibility of capturing the true breadth of the dynamics in the family drama he's put a mask on and called by another name? Have you read *The Leftovers* by Tom Perrotta? Or *The Unnamed* by Joshua Ferris? If not, I can tell you what they're about: families with problems who also have something really weird going on that acts as a sort of conductor for their problems, without which talking things through would be extremely difficult and possibly make for a story plagued by its own sappiness.

Owing to the Guest/Lurhmann dynamic, *Baby on Fire* sheds new light on the weirdness-on-account-of-fear-of-sappiness genre. Imagine Luhrmann's *The Great Gatsby* except that, for every music video-style sequence, there's a middle-aged white guy sitting off to the side talking about how much he hopes Gatsby will defeat Tom Buchanan and win Daisy's heart, because "if not for that, but for what purpose do parties serve?"

Baby on Fire is a little like that. On the one hand, you've got Luhrmann-style fireworks in the form of a baby that's literally burning while really good music plays. And on the other, you've got Guest-style commentary in the form of Gwen and Jed's total detachment from the very real problem burning away in their nursery. And through it all, yes, Gwen and Jed, with a baby burning in the next room, turning their whole house hot, will encounter domestic issues. What will they do with a baby they cannot hold?

Will their basic morning encounters in the kitchen become more strained? Will Gwen's flirtation with her tanned but superficial coworker become more salacious? Will Jed sound out the names of therapists in the Yellow Pages, check his online banking to see if he can afford one, and decide over and over again that taking a long, mopey walk down the bike path during which he smiles far too widely at dog walkers does him just as much good? Yes, in *Baby on Fire*, the domestic issues are still there. But, thanks to the Guest factor, they're marked by a peculiar self-awareness or possibly

extreme anti-self-awareness that, ultimately—baby flames aside—
leaves the whole family cold.

"This baby is going to burn itself down," Gwen says.

"We have encountered a major obstacle to happiness," Jed says.

"Our domestic issues are their own separate animal," Gwen says.

"I can't touch the thing. It hurts too much. Both my arms, and
my insides," Jed says.

"It hurts me that the ultimate object of our affection hurts
you," Gwen says.

"It hurts me that the ultimate object of our affection hurts me
and therefore hurts you," Jed says.

"We are in a closed loop," Gwen says.

"I wonder if we could just weep," Jed says.

"I can't believe a hot baby turned us cold," Gwen says. "We
could call it *Parents in Tears*," Jed says.

"I guess we could," Gwen says.

So that kind of thing goes on for a while, and then, the movie
has to end. And it does so with Jed and Gwen turning to ice
sculptures while standing within inches of their unnamed burning
baby. And the camera zooms in. And you see the heat flames
reflecting off the glassy ice.

And you wonder how we got to a point where this was possible.